THE ITALIAN KITCHEN GARDEN

JOANNA PONCAVAGE

Andrews McMeel Publishing

Kansas City

www.andrewsmcmeel.com

Library of Congress Cataloging-in-Publication Information

Poncavage, Joanna.
    The Italian kitchen garden / written by Joanna Poncavage.
        p.   cm.
    Includes bibliographical references (p.   ).
    ISBN 0–8362–3258–5(hd.)
    1. Cookery (Vegetables) 2. Cookery (Herbs) 3. Cookery, Italian.
    4. Vegetable gardening. 5. Herb gardening.   I. Title.
    TX801.P66 1997
    641.6'5'0945—dc21   97-15697
                                                            CIP

The Italian Kitchen Garden is produced by becker&mayer!

Cover photography by Michels Studio/Darren Emmens
Cover design by Trina Stahl and Heidi Baughman
Interior illustrations by Carolyn Vibbert
Interior design by Heidi Baughman
Production and layout by Heidi Baughman and Amy Redmond
Edited by Jennifer Worick

CONTENTS

General Gardening Tips 79

Appendixes 91

INTRODUCTION

I don't have any Italian ancestors, at least as far back as I can tell. The grandmother in the kitchen of my memory is Pennsylvania German, with a gift for cooking white foods and roots. But we lived on a farm and the fields were like fully stocked produce aisles, only longer.

Perhaps it all started with Romano beans. Even in their green bean stage, they're thick and rich and meaty, just like those Lazy Wives (pole beans, so called because they are stringless and easy to prepare) my grandmother liked. But Romano vines put out more beans, and so Lazy Wives were replaced. Or maybe it was the demographics of the coal towns in John O'Hara country where my grandparents sold their produce. When their customers wanted plum tomatoes and eggplants instead of potatoes and cabbage, they obliged. My grandmother found she had a gift for cooking eggplant and I ended up with a cosmopolitan palette.

And years later, a kitchen garden with a definite Italian accent. The farm gave me a taste for all kinds of vegetables, and no other cuisine glorifies vegetables the way Italian does. Living in New York City (where I checked cookbooks out of the public library by the bag as if they were groceries) taught me that vegetables you grow yourself taste better than any other vegetables in the world. Back in Pennsylvania, I vowed I'd never be hungry for fresh, home-grown vegetables again. Then I fell in love with garlic—how it grows, its colorful culinary history, its amazing health-giving properties. And since it can be difficult to find an Italian recipe that doesn't start with garlic, I became an Italian gardener and cook by default.

And that's what kitchen gardens are all about: close to the heart, close to the hearth, customized, and convenient. Now, whenever I need an ingredient, all I have to do is step outside and pick it at its peak of freshness and flavor. My kitchen garden is large enough to produce a nice range of things—basics I use every day, many of my favorite vegetables, herbs to savor, and flowers for the table!

Thanks to a number of American seed companies that specialize in real Italian vegetable varieties (they're listed on page 107), I'm growing small, tender lavender eggplants instead of the big, tough, deep purple kind. Zucchini with stripes and ridges. Long, sweet, frying peppers that caramelize when you cook them. Flattened little onions, and lettuce so red and frilly it looks like a rose. New World versions of these treasures can be found in any American supermarket, but if you want to experience the true tastes of Italy, you've got to grow the vegetables yourself.

Therefore, this book is mainly for the gardener. I've listed the vegetables and herbs indispensable to the true Italian garden, with detailed information on how to grow them. Also included is a chapter that covers gardening basics, such as siting the garden, laying out the beds, fertilizers, transplanting, mulching, trellising, and pest protection. You'll also find brief references to how Italian cooks might use each vegetable, recipes for enjoying your fresh-from-the-garden harvest, plus short notes on Italian wine, cheese, vinegar, and olive oil. I think you'll agree that for flavor and health, all roads lead to Rome!

THE MOST
ITALIAN OF
VEGETABLES

ARTICHOKES (*Carciofo*)

Artichokes (sometimes called "globe artichokes") are really the unopened thistly buds of a big, rangy plant that can grow up to five feet tall. These buds are usually pale olive green, but some varieties, especially those grown around Venice, are shaded a beautiful violet color. Very young buds are tender and completely edible. The outer portions of the leaves and the fuzzy inside "chokes" of older buds are tough and usually discarded.

Italians have as many ways with artichokes as Machiavelli had schemes. Artichokes have a mild, nutlike flavor, and they pop up everywhere: in antipasti, soups, salads, stuffed and baked in casseroles, or boiled and served with a dipping sauce. (An excellent uncooked green sauce, *salsa verde*, is made from finely chopped parsley, basil, chervil, capers, and lemon juice.) Sweet, tender, and tiny young artichokes are also sliced thinly and dressed uncooked with olive oil, salt, pepper, and lemon juice as a salad.

Artichoke plants are a bit of a challenge to grow, mostly because they are tender perennials that won't survive winter temperatures that remain below 20°F for long periods of time; they also don't like hot summers. Artichoke plants do best in moderate climates (cool winters, warm summers) where they can grow larger year after year. Most North American climates are too extreme for artichokes to thrive, but the coast of central and northern California has the perfect, mild, moist Mediterranean-like conditions for these plants. (In fact, Castroville, California, on Monterey Bay, is the "Artichoke Capital of the World.")

The Most Italian of Vegetables

Starting artichokes from seed is an inexpensive way to grow wonderful varieties, but some may not form any of those delicious buds until their second year. An exception is Imperial Star, a new California variety developed to produce lots of tasty buds the very first summer. Some varieties bud up earlier in the season than others: A beautiful purple-streaked Italian variety, Violetta, is among the first to produce buds each year.

Sow artichoke seeds in a container filled with an all-purpose seed-starting mix about two months before the last expected frost. Move plants into individual containers as they start to outgrow their first home. Move them into their permanent spots in the garden after danger of frost has passed.

Whether grown from root sections or from seedlings, artichoke plants will do best in loose, well-drained, fertile soil in a spot that receives a full day of sun. A raised bed is

an ideal location, because it will provide that very important good drainage. Set artichoke roots with their crowns just above the surface of the soil. Space plants or root sections at least 4 feet apart in all directions.

Plants grown from root sections or one-year-old artichoke plants should produce buds the first year they are planted in the garden. These starts can be purchased at many West Coast nurseries. They can also be purchased by mail. (See Seed and Plant Sources, page 107, in the appendixes.)

KEEPING IT GOING

Artichokes benefit greatly from a thick root-cooling mulch. A thick mulch will also keep their root zones moist. If you garden where it's not unusual for summer temperatures to reach the nineties, grow your artichoke plants in light shade.

Water artichokes heavily and regularly. They are big, thirsty plants. They get hungry, too. Feed them at least once a month by watering them with fish emulsion solution. Mulch with rich compost once or twice a year to provide additional fertility.

To improve their chances of winter survival in marginal areas, cut off the tops of the plants close to the soil in fall and mulch with a thick layer of straw.

PESTS AND DISEASES

Gophers, very common pests in western states, are especially fond of artichoke roots. To protect your plants, grow them inside an underground cage of fine mesh wire. If black aphids show up, hose them off plants regularly with a steady stream of water.

The Most Italian of Vegetables

HARVEST

Cut the buds from the plant anytime before they start to open. They should be firm to the touch. Buds are ready to eat as soon as they reach the size of a hen's egg. (If any artichoke buds become too large and tough to be eaten—a sad waste, but a possibility—allow them to open slightly to expose their pink, thistly center, then cut them so they have a long stem and dry them for decorative arrangements.)

ARUGULA (*Rucola*)

Arugula is a spicy green that adds a hottish, horseradishy taste to salads and sautés. A member of the mustard family, arugula is a relative of radishes and broccoli. In fact, its leaves look like miniature versions of broccoli leaves. Other names for arugula are "garden rocket," "roquette," and "rugula."

Legend has it that arugula grows wild throughout continental Europe and England because its seeds were spread by Roman soldiers hoping to be in one place long enough to harvest a cutting. (It's a fast-growing green.)

Arugula often gets the place of honor at the Italian table as the main topping on a very simple pizza: just arugula, olive oil, and a little cheese. It's also an indispensable addition to *mesclun*, a French mix of salad greens such as lettuce, radicchio, and green chicory that is common in northern Italy.

Some seed companies sell an arugula that is closer to the wild form of this pungent green. Look for words like "wild" or "rustic" or "rucola" in the seed catalog descriptions. This plant is more compact and less likely to bolt into flowering as the temperatures rise in summer.

GETTING STARTED

Arugula is a no-fail, quick-growing, cool-weather crop. Sow its seeds as early as you can in spring, about the time you sow those first-of-the-season vegetables such as radishes and peas. Prepare the bed until the surface is smooth and finely worked. Sprinkle the seeds as evenly as possible over the bed, aiming to have one every inch or so, and cover them with a thin (less than ¼ inch) layer of fine soil. Keep the seedbed moist, and the seeds will sprout in one to two weeks. Gradually thin the plants to about 6 inches apart.

You can also grow arugula in the cool days of fall. Just sow its seeds at least one month before your first fall frost if you garden where winters are frigid. In areas with mild winters, such as the Pacific Northwest, arugula can survive year-round.

KEEPING IT GOING

Arugula, like other leafy green plants, will do best in soil that has good amounts of nitrogen. So dig in a couple of inches of finished compost as you prepare arugula's spot in your garden. And because arugula will do even better in well-drained, nitrogen-rich soil, make that spot a raised bed.

Keep arugula well watered to prevent the plants from becoming stressed, which will cause them to flower and go to seed prematurely, or at the very least, to turn tough. Hot summer weather will cause arugula to flower, too. For a continuous supply of the most tender leaves, sow small quantities of seed every few weeks or so.

PESTS AND DISEASES

The only pest that might bother arugula is the flea beetle. This is a tiny, shiny, black bug you will see glistening on arugula's young leaves while it chews little holes in them.

(Mustard family plants, plus eggplant, are flea beetles' favorite fodder. If you plant them, they will come.) If flea beetles are especially pestiferous in your area, cover your bed of arugula with a floating row cover before the seeds sprout. Later, when the plants have grown, lift the row cover only to harvest leaves. You can also protect your plants by frequently washing off the flea beetles with a spray of water.

HARVEST

You can pluck the flavorful leaves of arugula anytime after the plant is several inches tall, or a month or so after sowing. As the weather warms, arugula will quickly shoot up to 3 or 4 feet tall and form pretty little white or pale yellow flowers. Eat lots of arugula *before* the plant flowers (and the weather turns hot), because that is when its leaves are the most tender and its taste is the most subtle. Old, tough leaves will taste harsh and brassy. However, arugula flowers are nicely edible and can be tossed into salads or strewn onto platters.

The Most Italian of Vegetables

ASPARAGUS (Asparagi)

Asparagus spears are the sweet, tender springtime shoots of a large perennial plant. If left uncut, these shoots will eventually develop into ferny foliage. Asparagus grows wild abundantly around the Mediterranean, where it has been eaten since the time of the Egyptian pharaohs, and probably before. Asparagus has been cultivated in Italy for centuries, and Tuscany, the province that lies along the upper west coast, has the reputation as the country's asparagus capital. It's here that cool winters and rich soils combine to produce thick, flavorful spears.

For cooking, asparagus spears are tied in bunches and placed upright in shallow boiling water in a narrow, covered container to steam. In this way, the delicate tips are protected and do not become overdone.

The classic seasoning for simply steamed asparagus is a little of the best olive oil and a squeeze of lemon juice or a few drops of vinegar. In Italy's north, steamed spears are topped with grated Parmesan, butter, and fried eggs to be served as a light springtime meal. In the south, asparagus is frequently mixed with pasta or sliced into soups, accompanied by garlic and shavings of sharp, hard cheese. For antipasto, it's rolled in thin crepes or slices of prosciutto, a fine dried, cured ham.

GETTING STARTED

American asparagus varieties are very similar to those grown in Italy. Any good, flavorful variety should do well in almost any region of North America, with the exception of the tropics or subtropics. Asparagus needs a winter period of dormancy for continued success. And because asparagus is a perennial plant, a well-tended patch can continue to produce succulent springtime spears for decades.

Asparagus is grown from bare root sections, called "crowns," that can be purchased readily from nurseries or mail-order catalogs. These root sections are best planted in early spring after danger of severe frost has passed.

Choose a site in full sun and with good drainage. Spread 1 to 2 inches of compost over the site and mix it deeply into the soil. Dig trenches about 1 foot wide and about 8 inches deep, and lay the asparagus crowns at the bottom about 18 inches apart. Spread out the roots of the crowns, making sure the growing points are right-side up. Cover the crowns with several inches of soil and rich compost, wait a week or two, then repeat this procedure until the trench is filled. Mound the soil over the trench slightly, then cover the surface of the bed with a thick organic mulch of leaves or straw.

KEEPING IT GOING

Keep the asparagus bed well watered but not overly wet. Asparagus benefits from a rich soil, so spread a couple of inches of compost over the bed every year to provide nutrients for the plants.

Renew the mulch at least once a year, too. Mulching also will help control weeds, which are very detrimental to

The Most Italian of Vegetables

good asparagus production. In cold climates, add more mulch to protect the asparagus bed in winter. In spring, pull back the mulch to allow the sun to warm up the soil.

PESTS AND DISEASES

To deter pathogens that can infect asparagus, choose a strong, disease-resistant variety, and plant it in a raised bed or other well-drained spot.

The main insect pest is the asparagus beetle. To deter beetles from overwintering in the garden, cut off the dead asparagus plants after the first hard frost, chop them up, and compost them in a hot pile.

HARVEST

Wait until the second year of growth before cutting a few spears from a new planting of asparagus. Allowing the roots to spread and strengthen will really pay off later. By the third year, the plants will be hardy enough for all their early shoots to be harvested.

Gather the spears by cutting them off gently just below the surface of the soil with a knife. Be careful not to slice into the hidden growing tips of spears-to-be. Asparagus spears are "ripe" when they are several inches tall; their tips should be tight.

When the sprouting spears become thin in diameter, they start growing almost faster than they can be cut, and their tips begin to quickly loosen into light foliage, it's time to give the asparagus patch a rest for another year.

BEANS (*Fagioli*)

Three very distinct types of beans are likely to be found in the kitchens of Italy: fava beans, green beans, and shelling beans.

Fava beans are native to the Mediterranean, and were grown in Italy long before the other two, which are recent immigrants from the New World. Fava beans are also called broad beans, or *aquadulce*. Shelled, they look like tan lima beans, but fava beans put lima beans to shame because they have so much meat and texture. Fava beans are extremely high in protein. Unlike the beans that are native to the Americas, fava beans grow well in cool weather.

In Italy, fava beans are a springtime treat, frequently eaten raw, straight from the pod. Fava beans and chicory, an ancient dish in Mediterranean culinary history, can be traced to Egypt and is traditional on the island of Sicily and in Puglia, the heel of Italy's boot. The beans are cooked and mashed into a purée and served with steamed chicory (a dandelion-like variety is traditional), fresh ground black pepper, lots of extra virgin olive oil, and sliced sweet red onion.

Italians like their green beans thick and hefty, not pencil thin or thinner like the *haricots verts* favored by the French. Most typical of the Italian green beans are the Romano varieties (you can buy the seeds of Romano bush bean or Romano pole bean, and there's even a yellow Romano bean). At the peak of edible ripeness, Romano beans will be 6 to 8 inches long, flat, and wide. The seeds inside the pod will be starting to show their rounded shapes,

The Most Italian of Vegetables

but the whole affair will be tender and stringless with a rich, nutty flavor. Other flattened beans you can grow for true Italian taste include Roma II (a hybrid bush Romano) and Golden Roma, with golden yellow pods.

Typical Italian dishes of green beans include a green bean and potato salad, and a Genoese combination of pasta, green beans, boiled potatoes, and basil pesto. In the south, green beans are cooked with garlic and tomato sauce. They are an indispensable ingredient in minestrone, and they can be marinated for antipasto or tied in bundles and dipped in egg and flour and fried in olive oil.

Shelling beans grow like typical green beans, but they are harvested later, when the beans inside the pod have hardened slightly and are full and flavorful. Then the beans are shelled from their pods and cooked up in soups or by themselves. (The beans, not the pods; the pods at this point are very tough and only fit for the compost heap.) Prepared at this stage (halfway between green bean and dry bean), the pale green or cream-colored beans cook quickly and have a wonderful fresh taste as well as a hearty, satisfying quality.

The Tuscan style is to cook fresh white beans until tender, dress them with garlic and sage sautéed in olive oil, then coat them in tomato sauce. Another popular combination forgoes the tomatoes, but adds one or two mashed anchovies.

In many seed catalogs you can find Italian-type shelling beans, including a variety called *Borlotto*, with pods that start out green but ripen into cream streaked with rose. Beans called *cannellone* mature into white kidney beans.

GETTING STARTED

Fava beans

Any fertile garden soil in full sun will do. Plant fava beans 1 inch deep and 2 to 3 inches apart in rows 2 to 3 feet apart; thin them to 4 to 6 inches apart within the row. The plants will grow 2 to 4 feet tall, and may need to be tied to stakes or a trellis to keep them from falling over.

Gardeners in mild climates such as the Pacific Northwest can sow favas in fall for overwintering. Gardeners in cold-winter areas should sow fava beans as early as possible in spring. Either way, the beans will be ready for harvest by late spring or early summer.

Green beans and shelling beans

Wait until all danger of frost has passed. Plant the seeds 1 inch deep and 2 to 3 inches apart in rows 2 to 3 feet apart; after seedlings sprout, thin them to stand 4 to 6 inches apart within the row.

KEEPING IT GOING

Nothing special here. Just keep beans well watered and weed-free, and you'll soon be richly rewarded.

The Most Italian of Vegetables

Fava beans

If fava beans start attracting black aphids (which will look like little black specks at the tips of the plants), wash the aphids off with a stream of water from the garden hose.

Green beans and shelling beans

The nemesis of *Phaseolus vulgaris* (the common garden bean) is the Mexican bean beetle. These are nasty little creatures that look like big, dull orange lady beetles. (Count their spots to tell the good bugs from the bad bugs. Lady beetles or ladybugs, because they are of various species, will have any number of spots on their backs, but the Mexican bean beetle always has sixteen.) Mexican bean beetles and their fuzzy yellow larvae will feed on the leaves of bean plants until the leaves look like lace.

Check bean plants daily and knock the slow-moving Mexican bean beetles and larvae off the plants and into a can of soapy water. Or put in a call for help: A number of beneficial insects, such as the spined soldier bug, prey on Mexican bean beetles. Attract beneficials to your garden by growing lots of flowers in or near your garden for pollen and nectar to feed them, and by installing some perennial beds to shelter them.

HARVEST

Fava beans

Pick fava beans when the pods are large and fully formed and the beans inside are plump and green—but the younger they are, the more tender and tasty they will be. You can start to harvest about two months after planting.

Green beans

Pods are ready for plucking when they are about ½ to ¾ inch wide and about 6 inches long. They should be flat and just starting to swell. Pick the pods regularly to keep the plant producing more beans. Hold the plant with one hand and gently pull the ripe beans away with the other. Be gentle, because a rough touch can damage the plant or pull it out of the ground. Don't harvest green beans while the plants are wet—this can cause an outbreak of fungal disease.

Shelling beans

Wait until the beans have filled out the pod and made it bumpy. To check for ripeness, break open a pod or two. The beans inside should be firm and full, and the moist interior of the pod should be starting to dry. Shuck the beans out of the pods, just like you would shell green peas.

(Note: You can let any of the above beans mature on the plant until they are dry and hard inside crisp pods. Crush the pods, sift out the beans from the debris, dry them thoroughly, and store them in airtight containers. The recipe of choice for dried beans is soup, and Italy has its sustaining ham and bean soup, made heartier with the addition of tiny pasta bits. Dried fava beans may have tough skins that need to be removed by blanching prior to cooking.)

BROCCOLI and CAULIFLOWER
(*Broccolo* and *Cavolfiore*)

Italian broccoli can be a slightly different vegetable from the heavy, dense, dark green heads sold in any American supermarket. Italians grow a lot of these modern hybrids, but they also plant broccolis that have smaller heads (sprouting broccoli) and a broccoli relative that is mostly leaves (broccoli raab).

Sprouting broccolis are bushy, leafy plants up to two feet or more tall. They will produce main heads that are from 3 to 6 inches across, plus lots of smaller shoots lower down on the stalk. (Broccoli "heads" are really clusters of tight little buds.) Italian Green Sprouting Calabrese broccoli is named for Calabria, the region that forms the toe of Italy's boot. *De Cicco* broccoli is another old Italian variety. Purple Sprouting broccoli has attractive purple-colored heads.

Broccoli raab is more a leafy vegetable than a "headed" broccoli. The whole plant is harvested and eaten—leaves, stems, buds, and little yellow flowers. It has a bitter, mustardy taste that mixes well with bland white beans and the nutty sweetness of toasted garlic. Broccoli raab is also a different species of *brassica* from the other broccolis (*Brassica rapa* as opposed to *Brassica oleracea*).

When Italians steam broccoli, they include some tender leaves and peeled stems as well as the florets. (Broccoli leaves and stems contain lots of vitamins.) Dressed with toasted garlic slices and a light olive oil and a splash of wine, steamed broccoli makes a hearty side dish or an elegant lunch. Broccoli, as well as other greens with a slightly bitter bite, are often used to fill calzone, which are pockets of pizza dough that are stuffed and baked.

Cauliflower, a close relative of broccoli, is prepared in many ways, too. It's common in mixed-vegetable dishes, breaded and fried, baked in white sauce, or tossed with pasta. Cauliflower as cooked in northern Italy is sautéed with garlic, parsley, and oil, topped with a little tomato sauce, and sprinkled with Parmesan cheese.

GETTING STARTED

Broccoli and cauliflower do best in a rich, well-drained soil. To prepare the garden for broccoli, dig in a 1-inch layer of finished compost or aged manure.

Broccoli and cauliflower are cool-weather crops that produce the biggest heads with the best taste if they can do most of their growing while temperatures are in the lower sixties. Hot summer temperatures cause broccoli and cauliflower to grow quickly and rush into the flowering stage. Hot temperatures can also make them taste bitter. For most of the United States, this means they are best grown as either a spring or a fall crop.

For spring crops, sow seeds for broccoli and cauliflower about ¼ inch deep in containers indoors about six to eight weeks before your last expected hard spring frost. For best germination, give them a spot that's warm (between 70° and

80°F). After the seeds have sprouted, move the containers into bright sunlight on a windowsill or under bright grow lights. Don't let them bake on the windowsill, though— the seedlings will grow best at temperatures between 60° and 70°F.

When the seedlings are about five weeks old, set them outside for an hour or so on a mild day. Gradually increase their time outside until they are toughened up slightly and large enough to go out into the garden. If broccoli and cauliflower are hardened off properly, they will be able to withstand a light frost, but if very cold spring temperatures are expected, protect the plants with fabric or plastic row covers.

Sow seeds of broccoli raab directly into garden soil at about the same time you plant radishes (another *brassica* that loves cool weather), or up to two months before the date of your last spring frost. When the seeds sprout, thin them so that the seedlings stand about 3 inches apart.

For a fall crop, sow heading broccoli and cauliflower seeds in midsummer in containers indoors, or in a cool spot outdoors; a spot that is shaded from afternoon sun works well. When the plants are several inches tall, move them to their permanent location in the garden. With only a little protection, they'll keep on growing and forming heads for a month or more after the first frost.

KEEPING IT GOING

Mulch your broccoli and cauliflower plants with a thick layer of dried grass clippings or straw to keep the soil around the plants cool and moist. Replenish this mulch as needed as it deteriorates. Don't let the soil around your plants dry out—give it a thorough soaking several times a week.

Broccoli and Cauliflower

Feed growing broccoli and cauliflower plants by watering them with a weak solution of fish emulsion, or by mixing in some aged manure or rich compost when you replenish their mulch. Foliar-feed the plants by spraying them with a solution of liquid seaweed extract to supply a dose of important plant minerals.

PESTS AND DISEASES

Keeping broccoli and cauliflower plants stress-free—that is, well fed, well watered, and cool—is the best prescription for minimizing pest problems. However, a couple of notorious insects can't resist these brassicas and may make an occasional appearance in your garden.

The easiest way to keep imported cabbage worms and cabbage looper caterpillars off the crop is to grow your broccoli and cauliflower under a floating row cover. Drape this light, airy fabric over young transplants as soon as they are set out into the garden (leaving some slack for them to grow into), and anchor the cover with boards along its edges to keep it from blowing away.

Another option for wormy pests is Bt (*Bacillus thuringiensis*), a naturally occurring bacteria that is fatal to caterpillars. It lodges in their digestive tracts and gives them the tummy ache to end all tummy aches. You can buy Bt preparations in various forms—apply it according to package directions.

Give heading broccoli and cauliflower plants plenty of room—set them at least 2 feet apart in all directions. Good air circulation around the plants helps deter aphids, tiny little plant juice-sucking pests that like to congregate in moist, protected leafy places.

Heading broccoli and cauliflower will be ready for harvest about sixty days after the young seedlings are planted outdoors in the garden. The heads of hybrid varieties can be up to 8 inches across, while sprouting types will be smaller. Whatever the size, look for a firm, solid texture. If the buds that form the heads of these vegetables are starting to open into little yellow flowers, the heads are past their prime.

Harvest sprouting broccoli by cutting off the main head with a diagonal slice. Sprouting broccoli plants will keep on producing little heads over a long season if you cut the main head when its buds are tight and young, and if you make the cut high up the stem. New sprouts will form along what's left.

You can harvest broccoli raab by cutting off its leafy tops as soon as the plant sends up flower stalks (and the earlier you cut the plants, the more tender and tasty the leaves and bud clusters will be). Lop off just the top half of the plant, and it will regrow for a second (and maybe third) cutting.

CHARD (*Bietola da Taglio*)

Chard, a member of the beet family, is especially popular in Greece and Italy. Chard is a hefty, vigorous plant that will send up long, narrow, crinkled leaves that can be 2 feet tall. These leaves have a crunchy central stem. The most authentically Italian chard has white stems and veins, but some chard has red ones and is sometimes called "rhubarb chard." There's even a golden chard.

Even though it's sometimes called "Swiss chard," this vegetable is truly an Italian favorite. Italian cooks chop it up and use it like spinach in omelettes and casseroles. Chard's long, wide leaves are also used to form little pouches stuffed with herbs, cheese, and bread crumbs, and poached in chicken broth.

GETTING STARTED

Chard will do best in a rich, loamy, well-drained soil that contains a good amount of organic matter. A thin layer of compost dug into the bed before planting should supply adequate fertility.

Sow seeds directly into the garden in spring, up to six weeks before the last frost is expected in your area. You can also plant chard late in the summer for a fall crop. Cover the seeds with ½ inch of soil in rows that are 18 to 24 inches apart. Thin the seedlings to stand 6 inches apart (toss the thinnings whole into salads).

KEEPING IT GOING

Give your chard planting lots of water when the weather is hot and dry. A thick layer of dried grass clippings tucked up

The Most Italian of Vegetables

under the plants makes a soil-cooling mulch for this crop that loves cool weather.

Like all leaf crops, chard benefits from a little extra nitrogen now and then. Water with a fish emulsion solution, or scratch some compost or a small quantity of a general-purpose organic fertilizer around the base of the plants. The nutrients they contain will be washed into the root zone of the chard plants each time you water.

HARVEST

Chard is a very prolific crop—a dozen plants, once they get going, should be more than enough for a small family. When the plant is about 6 inches tall, begin to harvest chard by cutting or breaking off the larger outer leaves. The small leaves left at the center of the plant will continue to grow and in turn will soon be ready for picking. This harvest can go on indefinitely if you don't cut below the central growing point of the plant.

If you get distracted by other garden bounty and your chard plants become overgrown, simply remove the tough outer leaves (a boost for your compost pile), harvest the more tender inner leaves, and wait for the tiny central leaves to grow.

Chard will grow lustily through the cool days of fall. It will even survive mild winters in many areas of North America such as the Pacific Northwest, the Middle Atlantic states, and the South. In colder areas, plants will make it through icy winters if you mulch them with straw and spread a floating row cover over the bed.

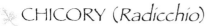

CHICORY (*Radicchio*)

Like lettuce, chicory is a very large category of leafy vegetables. Some chicories look like little round heads of lettuce, and some look like elongated heads of lettuce, almost like romaine. Some chicories are pretty little open rosettes, some grow leafy like cutting lettuce, and some have spiky, toothed leaves like dandelion. The vegetable Americans call "endive" is a chicory.

To further add confusion, some chicories are green, and some are red. In America, "radicchio" has come to mean chicory that is red instead of green, but in Italy, "radicchio" can refer to any chicory, red or green. (*Radicchio* is the Italian word for wild chicory; red chicory is *radicchio rosso*.) Some chicories start out green and their inner hearts turn red at maturity.

Red Treviso is a dependable, 300-year-old Italian heirloom chicory that looks like a small head of red romaine lettuce; its long, narrow leaves start out green, but turn deep burgundy with white veins as the weather cools. Grumolo chicory is a very cold-hardy variety common in the Piedmont region of northern Italy. Sown in mid- to late summer, the leaves form compact rosettes for harvest in late autumn through spring. There are dozens of other varieties to choose from, all authentically Italian.

Growing one or two varieties of chicory in your garden is an easy, elegant way to add taste, texture, and color to any salad—that's where you'll primarily find red and green chicory on the Italian table. It's also used as a garnish on a plate of antipasti.

Chicory has a clean, slightly bitter flavor that sweetens when it is cooked, in the way that garlic turns sweet and mellow when it is roasted. In Italy, chicories also are roasted, grilled, or sautéed, their tight little heads cut into quarters and drizzled with olive oil.

There are chicories for spring planting, and chicories for fall planting. Cold improves the flavor of this leafy vegetable; cold-hardy varieties will overwinter in most parts of the United States.

Spring chicory, like lettuce, is a cool-weather leaf crop, and chicory seeds can be sown in the same manner as lettuce seeds (see page 48). Also a leaf crop like lettuce, chicory will benefit from rich soil. Work an inch or so of aged compost or aged manure into the garden bed before planting.

For a spring crop, sow the seeds indoors about two months before the last frost. Seeds germinate best when the soil temperature is somewhere between 70° and 75°F. Set the young plants outdoors in a site that will receive full sun about one month later; they'll do their best growing while daytime temperatures are in the low sixties. A fabric row cover draped over young chicory plants will protect them from unseasonably cold temperatures. When temperatures turn hot at the peak of summer, spring-sown chicory will languish a little, but come fall, the plants will perk up and turn crisp and sweet.

Start fall crops of chicory anytime from midsummer on. Sow the seeds directly into a spot of garden soil that has been finely worked. If you garden where hot summer temperatures are the norm, sow the seeds in a protected spot that gets a little afternoon shade. When temperatures drop off slightly, move the young chicory plants from their nursery bed into full sunlight.

KEEPING IT GOING

Chicory tastes best when the plants haven't been stressed by drought, so water liberally and mulch the plants to keep their root zones moist. Feed chicory plants by spreading well-rotted compost around them at least once or twice during a season. The nutrients found in compost will be delivered to the root zone each time the plants are watered.

PESTS AND DISEASES

Chicory is virtually pest and disease free. The most important preventive measure is to space the plants far enough apart so that air can reach their leaves and dry them off after rain or watering. If leaves stay damp, rot and slugs may move in.

HARVEST

Many varieties of chicory are perennial—you can trim off their outer leaves or cut the head an inch or so above its central growing point, and the leaves will regrow. Give them a little mulch for winter protection, and they'll be back next spring.

EGGPLANT (*Melanzana*)

Native to India, eggplant was brought into Italy by traders. It could be argued that in Italy eggplant reaches its Nirvana, for what eggplant does best is blend with other flavors while lending them meaty substance and subtle undertones. Might not eggplant Parmesan be the world's most perfect combination? Garlic, olive oil, tomatoes, and cheese—all riding along on that humble but indispensable slice of eggplant to create a dish far more divine than the sum of its parts.

In Italy, perhaps because it soaks up olive oil like a sponge, eggplant is ubiquitous. It's baked in pies and pasta casseroles, served in sandwiches and salads, pickled for antipasti, and stuffed with bread crumbs, cheese, and herbs. To create *caponata*, the salsa of Sicily, chopped eggplant is sautéed and simmered with onions, tomatoes, and olives, seasoned with vinegar and capers, then served cold. In the north, eggplant is stewed with zucchini, peppers, and tomatoes in *ratatouille*, the classic side dish also common in southern France.

Although Americans are most familiar with big, purple, football-size eggplants, the varieties most common in Italy are narrower, dark violet teardrops, round lavender softballs, or sometimes smallish white eggs.

Violetta Lunga is a typical Italian variety with an 8-inch elongated shape. Its name simply means "long purple." *Violette De Firenze* is named for *Firenze* (Florence), the capital of Tuscany. It has a large oval shape and spectacular coloring—white at the top and lavender at the bottom, with the colors mixing into each other in the middle. *Rosa Bianca* is a pretty, lavender, easy-to-grow variety.

Eggplant needs a long, warm season to produce its best harvests. In the north, you may have to forgo the older heirlooms that can take up to ninety days to ripen, in favor of newer hybrids that can put eggplant on your table in sixty days or less. Don't worry—the taste and appearance shouldn't be too different.

Start tiny eggplant seeds indoors in containers up to eight weeks before it's time to move the plants into the garden, which will be a couple of weeks after the last frost date. Eggplant seeds need to be nice and warm for germination. Set them someplace where the temperature is eighty-something degrees (a box with an electric lightbulb inside it will provide the needed warmth), or use a heating mat.

As the eggplant seedlings grow, move them to larger containers, as needed. Wait until the soil is warm to the touch both day and night before you set the eggplants out into the garden. Eggplants should be the last vegetable you plant outside. They don't do much growing when temperatures are below 60°F.

Set young eggplant seedlings into a raised bed of fertile soil that contains lots of organic matter and that drains well.

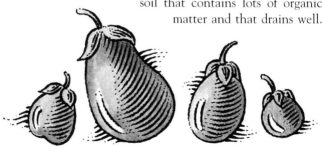

Give eggplants the warmest spot in your garden; a place in full sunlight in front of a heat-retaining stone wall would be ideal.

KEEPING IT GOING

Don't overfertilize young plants. Add compost to the soil before the transplants go in, but don't fertilize again until after the plant has flowered and fruit is beginning to form. Too much fertilizer before fruit set can cause the plant to produce leaves instead of baby eggplants. Be careful not to overwater an eggplant before it has formed fruits, also; too much watering too early can make an eggplant drop its flowers.

Once an eggplant begins to flower and set fruit, it will continue to do so, no matter how hot the weather gets. To keep them going, side-dress the plants with a rich compost or balanced organic fertilizer.

PESTS AND DISEASES

In most parts of the country, flea beetles are the insect that will cause eggplants the most problems. These tiny, shiny, jumping insects will show up as soon as you move the eggplants into their permanent garden spot. They love to eat eggplant foliage, and in serious infestations, will chew leaves until there's nothing left but holes.

Don't plant eggplants along the edge of your garden next to high weeds, shrubs, or trees—that's where flea beetles hide out when they are not chewing on your crops. (Flea beetles also love any kind of *brassica*, such as mustard, broccoli, or arugula.)

You can foil flea beetles by covering your eggplants with a generous amount of floating row cover the minute you set them into your garden. Allow enough slack cover for the plants to grow into, and, to keep flea beetles from sneaking in, make sure the row cover is anchored well with boards or rocks all the way around the eggplant bed.

HARVEST

The most important guideline for harvesting eggplant is to pick it before it becomes overripe. How can you tell? Eggplant is overripe if its skin has lost its shine and turned dull. Or if its flesh doesn't spring back when pressed with a thumb. Or if its seeds are crunchy and dark brown when you cut it open. Once an eggplant reaches this stage, it may taste tough and bitter.

Eggplant may be harvested at any stage before then—in fact, the younger it is when picked, the sweeter it will taste. And the more you harvest eggplant, the more fruit the plant will produce.

The Most Italian of Vegetables

FENNEL (*Finocchio*)

Fennel is a true Mediterranean native—it grows wild in all the countries that encircle this sea. Fennel has an ancient history as a medicinal plant, and its sweet, licorice-like taste has long made it a favorite food. A relative of celery and parsley, fennel looks something like a bunch of celery with a swollen, bulbous base. Fennel is low in calories and healthful, and even has an unofficial reputation as a "diet" plant—its sweetness can dull the compulsion to cheat.

The tender, pale, overlapping stalks that form this bulb are the most edible portion of the plant. Fennel stalks can be steamed, stewed, or braised to melting sweetness. A traditional Italian dish is fennel stewed in tomatoes, or fennel cooked in a white sauce and sprinkled with Parmesan. Fennel can also be sliced thinly into salads, as you would use celery, or marinated for antipasti.

The vegetable type of fennel that is grown for its tender, anise-flavored stalk is sometimes called "Florence fennel" or "sweet fennel" or, in Italian, *finnochio*. *Romy* fennel is an Italian heirloom that produces large, tender bulbs of refined texture.

Zefa Fino fennel, developed by the Swiss Federal Research Station, is commonly grown in northern Italy and throughout Europe. Its feathery leaves will stretch to 2 feet tall as the plant forms a large, oval-shaped bulb at the bottom of its stalks. Rudy is a new hybrid variety that is guaranteed to produce extra-large, heavy bulbs. Both are more resistant to bolting, that is, forming seeds prematurely, which interferes with bulb formation.

There are also a couple of types of fennel that are grown as herbs for their feathery, dill-like leaves and anise-flavored seeds. Bronze fennel is an herb type that can grow 6 or more feet tall and doubles as a beautiful gauzy ornamental. The sweetness of fennel adds marvelous grace notes to Italian sauce, counteracting the acid bite of tomato.

GETTING STARTED

Fennel is very easy to grow. It does best in well-drained, rich soil in full sunlight. It will tolerate a soil that is slightly acidic (see General Gardening Tips on page 79). In spring, sow the seeds thinly in a prepared bed where you want the plants to mature. Keep the seedbed moist but not soggy. The seeds will sprout in about twelve days. As the plants grow, water them regularly but moderately. Gradually thin the seedlings to stand about 10 inches apart in all directions. (You can cut up the immature plants into salads to enjoy little bursts of anise flavor.)

If you choose to start the seeds indoors, thin the seedlings after they sprout to one per container (peat pots work well), because you want to disturb the roots as little as possible when you set the seedling into the garden. Fennel is finicky about being moved—disturbing its roots might cause the plant to go to seed prematurely.

Sow some fennel seeds at periodic intervals throughout the spring and summer to have a nonstop supply of young, succulent fennel bulbs throughout the season. Fennel grows best when temperatures are in the low sixties, so if you garden where summers make tomatoes shrivel, skip the hottest part of the year and grow your fennel early or late in the season.

The Most Italian of Vegetables

KEEPING IT GOING

Fennel can easily survive mild winters (such as those on the West Coast or in the Middle Atlantic states) and continue to grow into next year. In their second year fennel plants send up flat, umbrella-shaped flowers that produce lots of seeds. When these seeds turn dry and brown and ripe, they will fall to the ground and sow themselves, giving you perhaps more fennel plants than you can handle. Simply pull up the baby plants that you don't want and toss them whole, roots and all (washed, of course) into your salad bowl.

PESTS AND DISEASES

Fennel is virtually free of pests and diseases, although there can be some rotting problems if drainage is not good and the plants are left in the garden too long.

HARVEST

Fennel is ready to eat as soon as its bulb grows to be a couple of inches across. To harvest, simply grasp the plant toward its bottom and pull, or use a garden fork to lift the plant out of the ground. Shake off the soil and trim off the roots and the tough stalks and leaves; wash the remaining stems and the bulb well.

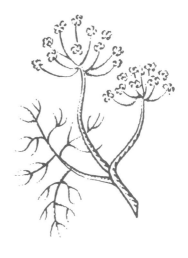

Fennel

GARLIC (Aglio)

Did Marco Polo really bring this most Italian of alliums back home with him on one of his return trips from China? It's pretty easy to think so. This pungent bulb, native to south-central Asia, but cherished by the world's great cuisines, can be found growing along the old trade routes from Europe to the Orient, seeded by caravan kitchen crews who more often than not were cooking in the dark.

Italian cuisine just wouldn't be the same without garlic. It's sliced onto pizza, minced into sauces, braised in stews, and pickled for antipasto. Garlic is a necessary seasoning in many fish, poultry, and meat dishes—it's the rare recipe that doesn't start with a clove or two of garlic. Real Italian garlic bread, called bruschetta, is first toasted, then rubbed with raw garlic, then drizzled with olive oil. Marinara-style tomato sauce is heavy with garlic and onions, the vegetables most likely to store best and longest on a sea voyage. And garlic is the main ingredient in spaghetti *aglio e olio* (spaghetti with garlic and oil).

Perhaps you've never considered growing garlic, but this is one vegetable that really turns into something else when it comes right out of your own garden. Fresh garlic is juicy, sweet, and aromatic, while garlic found in a supermarket is often old, acrid, and too strong.

The Most Italian of Vegetables

Believe it or not, there is more than one garlic variety to choose from. Skins can be silvery white, delicate tan, or streaked with rose or purple. Some garlics have many cloves per bulb, while some strains have bulbs with as few as four large, easy-to-peel cloves.

Some garlics grow with stiff but graceful flower stalks curving up from their centers, rising above their leaves, and dipping down again—these are sometimes called "serpentine" garlic, hardneck garlic, or *rocambole*. Garlic without a stiff stalk is called "softneck" garlic and is the best for braiding, although very nice decorative arrangements are possible with hardneck garlic, too.

Many garlics are named for their country of origin, and you can't go wrong with something like Chet's Italian or Italian White. Garlic with skin that is striped with purple is traditionally Italian, too, but any mild, full-bodied garlic such as Spanish Roja or California Early will do wonderfully well.

GETTING STARTED

Garlic is extremely simple to grow. Those cloves that you peel and slice to add heady, redolent flavor to so many dishes? Just stick a whole, unpeeled clove into the ground, and it will grow into a whole new head of garlic.

Fall is planting time—garlic is a cold-hardy plant that does most of its growing in springtime. When you plant it in fall, it spends the winter developing a good root system, which sets it in place to take advantage of those optimum growing conditions as the days start to warm up. Garlic should be planted around the time of the first fall frost. In the northern half of the United States, Columbus Day (the second Monday in October) is a good day for which to aim, but anytime in October will do. Gardeners in northern New England and Canada can plant garlic in late September. Southern gardeners can wait until November.

Garlic needs full sunlight and a good, rich, loose soil that drains well. A raised bed is an ideal spot. To plant garlic, carefully break up the heads of the seed garlic into cloves (don't peel them, and be careful not to bruise them). Next, dig a 3-inch-deep trench and press the garlic cloves, pointy-side up, into the bottom of the trench, about 4 inches apart. Fill the trench, covering the cloves with a couple of inches of soil. If you live in the northern half of the United States, lay down a thick mulch of straw or chopped fall leaves to protect the garlic in winter and to keep down weeds in spring.

KEEPING IT GOING

As well as good, rich soil to start with, garlic benefits from an occasional side-dressing of compost or blood meal when its leaves start to grow tall and green. An occasional foliar feeding of weak fish emulsion or liquid seaweed will nourish the plant, too. But once the leaves stop growing, don't fertilize anymore.

Do the same with water, too. Make sure your garlic has lots of water while its leaves grow, but when the tips of its leaves begin to brown, hold back on the liquids. Too much moisture at this stage weakens the bulb's outer layers of skin.

Keep your garlic patch free of weeds—the skinny leaves of garlic need all the sunshine they can collect. Replenish the mulch midseason if it starts to wear a little thin.

PESTS AND DISEASES

A great thing about growing garlic is that it has very few insect problems. In fact, growing garlic throughout your garden can help keep insect pests away from other, more susceptible crops. (And you know what they say about vampires…).

If you grow garlic in a raised bed that drains well, or in loose, loamy soil, you'll minimize the threat of fungal diseases. It also helps to avoid planting garlic in the same spot where onions or other garlic grew within the past three years. If you do harvest any bulbs that are soft and mushy and appear to be rotten, destroy them or banish them along with the household trash. Don't try to get rid of them by composting: it's likely that the disease spores won't be killed.

HARVEST

Along about July (perhaps earlier in the South), the tips of the leaves of the garlic plant will begin to turn brown. When about half of the leaves of the plant are brown, pull up a test bulb.

If your garlic is immature and not yet ready for harvest, it will have a thick, moist skin covering small, undeveloped cloves. Wait a few days and test again. It's important to harvest garlic at its peak of maturity—that is, when its individual cloves are rounded and bulbous, and the wrapper skin covering them is beginning to turn papery.

Garlic past its prime will have a weak, thin skin, and its cloves will be pushing through and starting to fall away from the bulb. Overmature garlic is quite edible, but it won't store for very long.

Pull your garlic on a day when the soil is on the dry side—muddy conditions can make for messy bulbs. Gently shake or brush off any clinging soil particles, and place the whole stalks in a shady, dry spot with good air circulation for about two weeks. This allows the skins sheathing the garlic bulb to dry out and tighten up, ensuring a capacity for long storage. After everything is dry, remove the outermost layer of bulb skin and chop off the long, dry leaves (unless you want to make braids—see page 105 for braiding instructions), retaining at least an inch or so of stem.

Garlic will last for months if you keep it in a cool, dry, airy spot. The coolest corner of your kitchen, porch, garage, or basement might do. *Do not* store garlic in the refrigerator—humidity levels are just too high in there, which may cause garlic to sprout.

KALE (*Cavolo Nero*)

Kale is a brassica. That is, it's related to that wide-ranging family with the spicy, sulfurous taste that includes broccoli, cauliflower, cabbage, brussels sprouts, radishes, and mustard.

Kale is grown for its leathery leaves, which in Italy are sautéed with a little olive oil and garlic, or sliced or shredded into soups or pasta. Kale's slightly bitter taste complements the sweetness of beans, too.

Kale plants are hefty and can grow 2 feet or more tall. *Lacinato* is an Italian heirloom kale with large, crinkled leaves of a beautiful dark blue-green color. Leaves of other varieties can be very frilly.

GETTING STARTED

All brassicas grow best in cool weather, and kale is no exception. It is traditionally planted as a fall crop, because as the temperatures drop, kale's flavor improves. Sow kale seeds outdoors in late summer. Space the seeds several inches apart in rows that are 2 feet apart. Keep the seedbed moist, and the seeds will sprout in three to ten days. Kale can also be planted in early spring as soon as the ground can be worked. Young plants will be tasty enough; just don't expect them to thrive in hot summer weather.

As the young plants grow, harvest some whole to give the remaining ones room to spread. Mature plants should stand about 2 feet apart. As all leaf crops, kale needs good amounts of nitrogen. Amend your soil with a couple of inches of finished compost or a thin layer of aged manure a couple of weeks before seeding.

KEEPING IT GOING

Spread straw or grass clippings around the bases of kale plants to keep their root zones moist and cool. If kale's leaves turn pale or start to yellow, feed the plants with a solution of fish emulsion or liquid seaweed. A side-dressing of compost will supply nutrients, too. Regular watering keeps kale's leaves sweet and tender.

PESTS AND DISEASES

Kale is remarkably unbothered by insects and germs, especially if you grow it stress-free by supplying adequate nutrients and moisture.

If aphids threaten the kale plants, simply hose them off with a stream of water. If flea beetles are serious problems in your area, throw a floating row cover over your kale patch as soon as you seed it. Your seedlings will sprout and grow unbothered by bugs.

HARVEST

You can cut the leaves of kale any time, but don't slice into the tiny leaves in the plant's center, which is its growing point. Harvest from the outside, removing the largest leaves first. And harvest often, because kale is most flavorful before its leaves are tough and overmature.

Kale grows well in cool weather, and, in fact, tastes best after a mild frost has touched its leaves, turning them sweet. You can even harvest it from under a snowdrift. Certain cold-hardy varieties can easily last for several seasons in most of North America. Just keep cutting, and kale will keep growing.

LETTUCE (*Lattuga*)

Italian salads are very plain and are eaten at the end of an Italian meal, the course before fruits and dessert. A typical salad might consist entirely of buttery soft lettuce leaves decorated with shredded *radicchio*, slivered carrots, and a few garbanzo beans. In summer, tomatoes and cucumbers are added. The dressing is do-it-yourself oil and vinegar.

Such simplicity demands fresh-from-the-garden excellence, and Italians grow a wide variety of lettuce types. One of the most popular is even named for their capital city and former empire: Romaine. They also grow butterhead lettuces with soft, loose heads kissed with red around the tips of their

leaves, or speckled with red throughout. One typically Italian lettuce is the soft, loose-leafed *Lollo Rossa*, which translates as "lazy redhead." Its big, frilly, tightly crinkled leaves are a dark burgundy in color.

Cutting lettuce (*da taglio* in Italian) is leaf lettuce that is grown to be cut when it is only a few inches high. Cutting lettuce is an important component of what northern Europe calls *mesclun*, a mixture of greens in a variety of tastes, colors, and textures. There's an Italian version of *mesclun* called *misticanza*, a traditional Piedmontese salad mix of lettuces and chicories in a variety of leaf shapes and colors that are seeded and grown together in the same bed. All the cook needs to do is clip the leaves into a bowl and pass the olive oil and grated cheese—it's a premixed salad.

GETTING STARTED

Lettuce is a cool-season crop; most varieties do best when grown early in the cool weather of spring or late in the season in fall.

You can start seeds of heading lettuces indoors four to eight weeks before frost ends in your region. Sow the seeds sparsely about 1 inch apart, and cover them thinly; keep the seed-starting medium moist but not soggy. After the seeds sprout, place their containers in a cool, bright spot.

When the seedlings are a couple of inches tall, transplant them outside in their permanent bed. This can be done before the last frost of spring, especially if you cover the plants with a floating row cover at night. If extra-cold weather threatens, lay a thin sheet of plant-protecting plastic over the row cover, too.

The Most Italian of Vegetables

Lettuce seeds can be sown directly into the garden up to a month before the last spring frost. (Lettuce seeds will germinate even when temperatures are in the forties.) Sow the seeds sparsely, and gradually thin the seedlings until the remaining plants are 8 to 12 inches apart. An option is to sow the lettuce seeds more thickly in a row, then transplant the seedlings to grow 8 to 12 inches apart as soon as they are large enough to handle.

Cutting lettuce seeds can be sown thickly across a small area. Sprinkle on the seeds so that they are spaced about ½ inch apart in all directions. Cover lightly, and keep the seedbed moist as the little lettuce plants sprout and grow.

KEEPING IT GOING

Like other leafy vegetables, lettuce needs good amounts of nitrogen. Before the young lettuce plants or seeds go into the garden, enrich the soil with aged manure or compost. After the lettuce plants are growing, an occasional spray of compost tea or liquid seaweed solution will supply important minerals. And lettuce stays cool and crispy if it receives lots of water.

For a nonstop lettuce harvest, sow small quantities of seed each week, to grow as many plants as your family can eat on a weekly basis.

If you live in a very hot climate, or as spring turns to summer, tuck lettuce transplants into the shade of taller crops like corn or pole beans. Just a little protection from the high, hot sun can keep lettuce cool and tender. Another option is to grow lettuce under a shade cloth, available at garden centers.

PESTS AND DISEASES

One of the best defenses against insects and fungus diseases is to space individual lettuce plants far enough apart so that they don't touch and air can circulate all around their leaves. Don't give aphids or fungal spores a damp, close place to hide!

Mulch lettuce with light straw or dried grass clippings to prevent disease-causing organisms from splashing up on the leaves from the soil.

HARVEST

Lettuce can be harvested at any stage of growth—the smaller the leaves, the more tender and delicate the salad will be. Of course, if a head of lettuce is your goal, you must wait until the plant folds its leaves into a crispy central bundle. In the meantime, however, you can pluck off a few of the larger outer leaves while you wait for the central head to form.

Cutting lettuces can be harvested when only a few inches high. But whenever you cut, don't cut too close to the ground or you'll take off the part of the plant from which the leaves sprout. Leave this central growing point intact, and your lettuce patch will send up a second, or even a third, crop.

Letttuce sown in spring will send up a flower stalk and begin to form seeds when temperatures start to climb into the upper seventies and above. Its leaves become tough and bitter, too. Unless you want the plants to complete their reproductive cycle by providing lots of free seed for your next crop, send these plants to the compost pile.

The Most Italian of Vegetables

ONIONS (*Cipolle*)

Traditional Italian onions are sweet, mild, and medium-size. They can be yellow, red, or white, and sometimes have a shape other than round. The Tropea area in Calabria has a particularly sweet large red onion. Onions are indispensable to Italian cooking, especially in the southeast, where they are used more than garlic. Every Italian region has an onion specialty, from the onion soups of the north to the onion pizzas of the south.

Italian *cippolini*, which translates as "little onions," look like squashed globes, about 2 inches across and 1 inch thick, with firm flesh and sweet, robust flavor. Red and yellow versions are available. Traditionally they are served whole, braised in a sweet and sour sauce or pickled. *Cippolini* are the perfect size for kabobs, too. Larger onions are often stuffed with a savory filling and baked.

Another typically Italian onion is sometimes called a "bottle" or "torpedo" onion. These are about 5 inches long and about 1½ inches in diameter. Two varieties of this type are Italian Red Torpedo or Red Florence; their cylindrical shapes make them excellent choices for slicing thinly into salads.

GETTING STARTED

When you buy onion seed, pay attention to whether the variety is a long-day or a short-day type. Onions are sensitive to day-length changes that trigger bulb formation. "Long day" onions are best grown in the north; "short day" onions are for the south. True Italian heirlooms are long-day onions that do best if planted in the northern half of North America, but you can probably find short-day versions of them, too.

Onions can be sown outdoors in a finely prepared seedbed as soon as the ground can be worked in spring. Onion seeds can germinate at 40°F, although they will do so more quickly at temperatures above 50°F. Cover the seeds with ¼ inch of fine soil and keep the seedbed moist. Thin or transplant the seedlings to be 4 inches apart in all directions.

You can give onions a nice early start by sowing their seeds in flat containers indoors at least one month before planting them out in the garden (two months is better in cold-winter regions). A loose, coarse medium with lots of perlite (a lightweight material available in garden stores) and sand will work best. Sow seeds four to the inch in narrow rows, and cover them with ¼ inch of fine starting medium. Transplant onion seedlings outside anytime after the snow melts and the garden soil can be prepared.

The Most Italian of Vegetables

KEEPING IT GOING

Onions need lots of nitrogen early in their growing cycle, so amend their garden bed by digging in an inch or so of rich compost or aged manure before planting seeds or transplants. This will allow the plants to develop strong, healthy leaves, which in turn will form nice big bulbs.

Water is a very important element for onions—they need regular doses of it because their root systems are small and shallow. Lots of water will help them grow large and juicy, and will also lessen the threat of pests and diseases by preventing stress on the plant. Cut back on water as harvest time nears, however, to cut the risk of fungus around the bulb and to optimize storage time.

Keep onion plants well weeded—their narrow leaves are poor competitors for sunlight's energy.

PESTS AND DISEASES

Onions are a relatively pest- and disease-free crop, especially if they aren't planted in the same spot year after year. Varying planting sites breaks the cycle of disease from one year to the next. It's important to clean up onion leaves and debris from the garden, too, to remove any onion pests attempting to overwinter.

If root maggots are a problem (they tunnel into the bulbs and cause them to rot), cover onions with a floating row cover as soon as they are planted outdoors. The cover will keep the onion fly from laying the eggs that will hatch into root maggots. Thrips are very tiny insects that feed on onion leaves and leave behind silver streaks on the green. You can wash thrips away with regular showers from the garden hose.

HARVEST

Onions can be pulled and enjoyed at any stage, from skinny scallion to bulbous green onion to fully mature globe. If you want to store onions for any length of time, however, you've got to wait until the plant matures and its juicy bulb is protected by a natural wrapper of dry, papery skins.

When an onion stops growing, its top falls over. When about half of the tops in your onion patch have fallen, pull all the onions and lay them on top of their garden bed for a couple of days to dry. Then gently clean them up by brushing off any soil clinging to their skins, and move them to a cool, dry, shaded spot for another few days to finish curing. When the onion's outer layers and necks are dry, trim off their roots and braid them. (See page 105 for braiding instructions.) Hang the braid in a cool corner of the kitchen for easy access—and because onions are very decorative.

The Most Italian of Vegetables

PEPPERS (*Peperoni*)

What's an antipasto without pickled peppers? The story with peppers is the same as with tomatoes—they are New World natives that were taken in by the Italians like long-lost relatives. All kinds are grown and used, from the sweet bell peppers to the longer, sweet frying types to small, red-hot cayenne and cherry types.

Peperonata is a savory Sicilian stew of sweet bell peppers cooked with lots of onions, olive oil, and green olives. It's served as a hot or cold relish, or added to other recipes as a flavoring. Sweet bells are often served stuffed, too; pine nuts, raisins, capers, and anchovies make up a classic filling.

Peperoncini are thin-walled, slightly spicy peppers that ripen from pale green to red. *Peperoncini* are usually pickled and served with antipasti. Hot cherry peppers, which look like little apples, also get pickled or stuffed with meat or a combination of bread crumbs, olives, capers, and anchovies. Skinny, extremely hot cayenne peppers are dried and ground up for red pepper flakes to flavor pastas and pizza.

At the pinnacle of pepperdom in Italy are the long, slender frying

peppers. Unlike America's green bell peppers, Italian frying peppers are sweet without a hint of bitterness. One of the most characteristic is called *Corno di Toro,* which translates as "bull's horn," because it really does look like one—up to 12 inches long, narrow, and tapered. Green at maturity, Italian frying peppers ripen to an even sweeter red or yellow. Their skins are very thin and tender.

Italians will make a meal out of peppers, frying them up at lunchtime with olive oil and garlic, cooking them very slowly so the sugars of the peppers caramelize. With a little grating of cheese, served with bread and a sparkling wine—paradise!

GETTING STARTED

Peppers are extremely easy to start from seed. Sow them indoors in individual peat pots six to eight weeks before setting them out in your garden. Fill the peat pots with a fine, light seed-starting mix, then drop one pepper seed in each. Cover the seeds lightly, water them well, and place the containers in a warm spot. At 85°F, peppers will germinate in one to two weeks' time. After they sprout, move the containers to a brightly lit but cooler spot; pepper plants grow best when temperatures hover around 70°F.

Water seedlings well, but avoid overly wet conditions. Feed them every week or so with a weak solution of fish emulsion. As the weather warms, place the seedlings in a sunny spot outdoors for gradually longer and longer periods of time. When garden soil temperatures reach the sixties (usually a couple of weeks after the last frost), plant the seedlings into the garden. If temperatures threaten to fall below 40°F, protect pepper plants with cardboard boxes or other coverings.

The Most Italian of Vegetables

A thin layer of compost dug into the soil before planting should supply all the fertilizer your pepper plants need. Don't apply large quantities of fertilizers that contain high amounts of nitrogen, because too much nitrogen will produce a pepper plant with lots of leaves but little fruit.

KEEPING IT GOING

When pepper plants are small, stick a simple wooden stake into the soil close to their main stem and tie the stem to the stake with soft twine or a strip of cloth. This will keep the plant upright during wind and rain. As its branches bend down under the weight of ripening peppers, tie them to the stake for support, too. An upright shape also improves the growth of the plant and improves yields.

Water growing pepper plants well, but try to keep their leaves dry to avoid the spread of fungus diseases. Mulch beneath the plants with a layer of grass clippings or other material to keep the root zone cool and moist.

Peppers are perennial plants and will keep on growing and producing as long as temperatures are warm. To prolong the growing season, cover pepper plants with a floating row cover when nighttime temperatures start heading down below the fifties.

PESTS AND DISEASES

If plants are grown too close together and it rains a lot, the peppers may develop rotten spots due to wet conditions. Make sure to space the plants far enough apart so their leaves can dry as quickly as possible.

The European corn borer is an insect that often infests a pepper planting. The troublesome stage is the larva, a

1-inch white worm with a dark head. After the European corn borer moth (the adult stage) lays its eggs on the pepper plant, the eggs hatch and the tiny larvae chew their way inside the pepper, where they feed and grow larger.

There are three ways to battle the borer. (1) Apply a *Bacillus thuringiensis* product when the moths are aloft and laying their eggs. These products are available in garden centers. The active ingredient is a bacteria that kills caterpillars. (2) Attract the borer's natural enemies by growing flowering herbs. (See General Gardening Tips, page 79, for more information.) (3) Grow peppers under a floating row cover to exclude the egg-laying moth.

HARVEST

Peppers reach their first stage of maturity when their green fruit attains full size and ceases to grow larger. Peppers are eminently edible at this stage, but wait two to three more weeks, and they will be fully ripe. Their color will change from green to red or yellow or orange, depending on the variety, and their taste will be much sweeter.

The Most Italian of Vegetables

SPINACH (*Spinacio*)

Italians grow many varieties of spinach, from the kind with deeply crinkled leaves, to the kind with flat, smooth leaves. They eat a lot of it, too—often as a simply steamed green seasoned with garlic, raisins, and pine nuts, and served alongside grilled meat. Sometimes spinach is steamed, then sautéed with olive oil and garlic.

Then there's *sformato di spinaci*, or spinach mold, an egg custard containing spinach, onions, and cheese. To Americans, this might be a main dish or a light lunch; in Italy, it comes somewhere in the middle of an eight-course meal, between antipasti and *dolci*.

Spinach also flavors and colors fresh green pasta, or *pasta verde*. Spinach mixed with ricotta, Romano, and Parmesan cheeses forms a rich stuffing for ravioli served in a

cheese–tomato sauce. Spinach also is a popular ingredient in dumplings (*gnocchi*), and spinach mixed with eggs, cheese, and garlic is often baked in a pie crust.

GETTING STARTED

Spinach grows best in cool weather when day and nighttime temperatures are somewhere close to 60°F. You can sow spinach seeds in early spring, up to two months before your last expected frost. Choose a spot with rich, loose soil.

Sow the seeds sparsely, one or two per inch in rows at least 1 foot apart. Keep the seedbed slightly moist, and the seeds will quickly sprout. As they grow, gradually thin the plants to stand from 2 to 6 inches apart. (The tiny plants you pull are eminently edible—add them whole to salads.)

For a fall crop, sow the seeds in late summer about two months before your first fall frost. If the weather in your region is still hot, sow the spinach seeds in a shady garden spot behind a taller crop destined to be removed soon.

Although it's a little labor-intensive, you can start spinach seeds in individual containers in a cool spot indoors, let them grow for a couple of weeks in a cool but brightly lit spot, then transplant them into your garden when temperatures cool to the sixties. You can harvest until the snows come, and next spring when the snows melt, you should have spinach plants all set to keep on growing.

KEEPING IT GOING

As a leafy green, spinach benefits greatly from additional fertilizing as it grows. Scratch in a little compost between rows of spinach, and water in the nutrients. Watering the

The Most Italian of Vegetables

plants occasionally with a fish emulsion solution also supplies nutrients to help them keep producing.

If you really like spinach, consider growing a variety famous for standing up to the heat of summer without bolting into seed. One of the most heat-tolerant is Italian Summer.

PESTS AND DISEASES

Spinach plants will stay healthy and fungus-free if they have lots of room to grow, so don't crowd them. If necessary, start thinning the plants soon after sowing and don't stop until adjacent, fully mature plants barely touch each other.

Sowing spinach in a raised bed is another great way to fight fungus—a raised bed drains well and siphons off unneeded moisture that can foster fungal growth. Don't water spinach on a cool, cloudy day or in the afternoon or evening of any day—fungus can start to grow on leaves very quickly.

Slugs, which often feed on spinach leaves, thrive in moist conditions, too. In addition to keeping your plants dry, surround your spinach patch with slug-repelling materials, such as sharp gravel, crushed eggshells, or other abrasives.

HARVEST

Harvest established spinach plants by pinching off the large outer leaves without disturbing the central growing point of the plant. The plants will keep growing and producing more leaves until heat or cold puts an end to them.

SQUASH (*Zucchino*)

Italians have a way with squash, and no Italian garden is complete without a couple of kinds. After all, zucchini is an Italian word for "summer squash"; so are *cocozelle* and *zuchetta*. Italian summer squash can be narrow and dark green, just like American zucchini. It can also be narrow with long, light green ridges, or very long and skinny and pale green. There's even a climbing, vining summer squash, *Zuchetta Rampicante*, which produces 15-inch curving, S-shaped fruits.

The old Italian heirloom summer squashes have a denser, nuttier, and creamier taste than modern zucchini hybrids. They won't become as soft as zucchini when cooked, either.

In typical simple cooking style, Italians often cut narrow squash in half lengthwise and bake them, drizzled with olive oil and garlic. Another version is to sauté thin zucchini slices in olive oil until brown, then marinate them in a garlic vinaigrette before serving at room temperature. Squash also are stuffed with bread crumbs, Parmesan cheese, and herbs. There's also a squash soup that dates back at least to the Renaissance.

In Italy, baked squash blossoms stuffed with ricotta cheese aren't a gourmet dish—they are common fare. Squash blossoms are also dipped in a very light batter and sautéed very quickly, or shredded and simmered with garlic, olive oil, and wine as a pasta sauce. Tiny little zucchinis are sold with their still crisp flowers attached, for steaming or sautéing all in one piece.

The Most Italian of Vegetables

GETTING STARTED

Squash is a warm-season vegetable that doesn't appreci-
ate transplanting, so wait
until the soil is warm, a
week or two after the last
springtime frost, before sowing
the seeds out in the garden where
they are to grow. Amend the soil by digging in a couple of
shovelfuls of mature compost or aged manure first. Squash is
one hungry vegetable that will thrive on all the minerals
and nutrients it can get.

If it's a bush variety (the seed catalog or seed packet
should tell the growth habits of the particular variety), sow
three or four seeds together in a hill about 2 feet across.
Space the hills at least 4 feet apart. You can also sow bush
varieties in rows. Sow the seeds 1½ inches deep and 1 foot
apart in rows that are 4 feet apart.

If the squash is a vining type, consider growing it up a
fence or trellis. Sow the seeds 1½ inches deep up to 1 foot
apart near the bottom of the structure, and as they grow, tie
the vines to it (or simply nudge them in the right direction).
Vining squash usually has whiplike tendrils at its tips for
grasping and pulling itself up and along.

Besides being a very Italian thing to do, growing vine-
type squash vertically improves the health of the plant
by improving air circulation around it. Growing vertically
also increases yields by exposing more of the squash leaves
to sunlight. In addition, the squash themselves will
grow nice and long and straight as they hang down from
the vines.

KEEPING IT GOING

Summer squash plants will obligingly produce more squash if they are picked regularly and often. Once an overlooked fruit begins to turn hard, the plant goes into its seed-producing stage rather than a flower-and-fruit mode.

PESTS AND DISEASES

Give squash plants lots of water. They'll produce higher yields of better-tasting fruit. What's more, when they are stressed by drought, plants are also susceptible to damage by insects and disease.

If insects such as squash bugs, squash vine borers, and cucumber beetles are an extreme problem, consider growing bush squash under a floating row cover to keep the pests off the plants, at least for the first part of their lives. Just be sure to allow enough of this light fabric for the plants to grow into. (See General Gardening Tips on page 79.) Remove the row covers when female flowers appear (the ones with bulbous swellings between the blossom and the stalk), to allow pollinating insects to visit the flowers.

HARVEST

Summer squash can be picked anytime, starting when they're extremely young (remember those squash blossom recipes?), but they will be most moist and flavorful before their seeds begin to toughen and mature. To harvest squash, cut the stems of the squash with a knife; pulling them off is likely to damage either the squash or the plant. Summer squash will keep only a few days in the refrigerator before they start to wilt (and very young squash will begin to wilt right away), so it's best to harvest squash just before cooking.

The Most Italian of Vegetables

TOMATOES (*Pomodori*)

Tomatoes are relative newcomers to Italian cuisine, having been grown in the Old World only for the past 500 years. Tomatoes are tropical plants native to Central and South America, and were introduced to Europe by returning Spanish explorers. The pastas and pizzas of Italy were waiting.

The earliest cookbook known to contain tomato recipes was Antonio Latini's *Lo Scalco alla Moderna*, published in Naples in 1692. His recipe for tomato sauce contains roasted tomatoes, minced onions, and hot chile peppers, with a little thyme, salt, oil, and vinegar. It could be the mother of all ketchups.

Italians call tomatoes *pomodori*, or "golden apples," because the first tomatoes to reach Italian shores were round and yellow. Other colors and shapes soon followed. Today Italians make good use of all kinds of tomatoes in all kinds

of ways, fine-tuning them with herbs and other vegetables. *Arrabiata* is the name for tomato sauce made "angry" with the addition of hot peppers. *Marinara* sauce contains onions and garlic, two ingredients sailors (mariners) were likely to have on board.

One of the most princely combinations is simply juicy slices of tomato overlapped with thick slices of the best mozzarella, drizzled with olive oil, sprinkled with fresh basil leaves and freshly ground pepper. Let it mellow at room temperature for an hour or so, then ravage it, armed with a loaf of fresh bread. A very common dish—a version of bruschetta—begins with toasted bread rubbed with fresh garlic cloves, then with quartered tomatoes, leaving as much tomato pulp on the rough bread as possible. Some droplets of olive oil and shreds of herbs finish this appetizer/snack, the ingredients varying according to local tastes and specialties.

The most Italian of tomatoes are oblong paste tomatoes with names like Roma, San Marzano, Milano, and San Remo. Some paste tomatoes with an Italian past are huge and heart-shaped, such as Giant Oxheart or Sicilian. All paste tomatoes have thick, meaty flesh that quickly cooks up into a heavy sauce. In southern Italy, puréed tomatoes are slowly dried into a thick, leatherlike paste in shallow bowls beneath the intense Mediterranean sun.

Other, equally Italian tomatoes are ribbed and irregularly shaped. Costoluto Genovese tomatoes have thick, meaty walls—cut them crosswise and you'll expose empty hollows instead of juicy seed cavities. Tomatoes like these beg to be stuffed with a mixture of bread crumbs, herbs, and cheese.

Principe Borghese is a variety of the type that is traditionally grown to be dried. These 2-inch egg-shaped tomatoes grow in clusters on tall, vigorous plants. Southern Italians simply pull up whole plants of red, ripe tomatoes and hang the plants on stone walls in the hot sunlight. (See page 105 for tomato-drying instructions using an oven or food dehydrator.)

GETTING STARTED

Tomato plants have either a bush shape or a vine habit. The bushy type tomatoes are called "determinates." Vining tomato plants are called "indeterminates." If you have a small garden, consider growing the determinate types, or be ready to train one or two indeterminates up a very tall trellis.

Tomatoes are tropical plants, and they are *very* easy to grow from seed. About four to six weeks before the last frost date for your area, sow tomato seeds in containers filled with a seed-starting mix. Set the containers on a tray in a sunny windowsill, keep the mix moist but not soggy, and tomato seedlings will sprout before you can say *"arrivederci."*

If plants are extra vigorous, you may need to move them into larger containers before setting them out into the garden. Check the roots by unpotting one plant. If a lot of roots are pressed against the side of the rootball, it's time for a change.

Wait until all danger of frost has passed before giving tomato plants their permanent outdoor home. Give them a site in full sun in rich, but not too rich, soil. Dig 1 to 2 inches of compost into the bed before transplanting, but don't overfeed the plants with a nitrogen-rich fertilizer. Too much of this nutrient will make a tomato plant produce a lot of leaves but little fruit.

All tomatoes, whether bush or vine, will benefit greatly from the support of a cage, stake, or trellis. Tie the vines to the support with soft twine or strips of fabric. Supporting structures will keep the plant from sprawling along the ground, thus improving ripening and protecting the fruit from rotting. The larger the plant, the bigger and stronger the support should be.

KEEPING IT GOING

Give tomatoes lots of water. A thorough soaking is best, rather than shallow showers more frequently. Mulch the plants with a thick layer of straw or leaves to keep the soil around the roots moist between waterings.

PESTS AND DISEASES

Plant tomatoes in well-drained soil (raised beds are ideal) and give them lots of room. A dry, airy environment lessens the threat of fungal and bacterial disease, and also deters aphids and whiteflies from colonizing the plants.

Tomato hornworms are large green caterpillars that can quickly eat many tomato leaves, leaving bare stems. If you find one of these creatures among the vines, send it to the guillotine. If it has little white bumps on its back that look like grains of rice, however, simply move it away from the tomato vines and wait—its days are numbered. Those white nodules are the cocoons of tiny parasitic wasps that will soon hatch into more caterpillar-killing wasps. (See General Gardening Tips on page 79 for more on how beneficial insects help control vegetable pests.)

THE MOST
ITALIAN OF
HERBS

The generous use of herbs is one of the hallmarks of true Italian cooking, and no Italian kitchen is complete without a full selection. Italians, specialists in adding extra flavor in any way possible to every recipe, rely on herbs to boost the ordinary to the sublime. Most of the herbs listed in this chapter are native to the Mediterranean area, and they've been in Italian kitchens since kitchens were caves.

All herbs are easy to grow—all they need is well-drained, weed-free soil. Hold back on water and fertilizer, and their essential oils will be more concentrated. (See How to Dry Herbs on page 105 in the appendixes.)

The Most Italian of Herbs

BASIL (Basilico)

There are dozens of different kinds of basil, varying in size, leaf shape, color, and flavor. All of them have the same characteristic mint/clove undertones, and all of them are wonderful for preparing pesto, the classic Italian combination of basil, garlic, aged grated cheese, olive oil, and pine nuts. Around Genoa, pesto's ancestral home, it's served as a dollop in a bowl of minestrone, and as a sauce for pasta or potato *gnocchi* (little soft mashed potato dumplings).

The most common type of basil is sometimes called "sweet basil." This type will form bushy plants several feet tall with many leaves and succulent stems. Some basils have crinkled leaves, and some have purple leaves. "Globe basil" is so called because it stays a cute 10 inches tall and forms round little bushes of small, thick, light green leaves. (Globe basil is perfect for making a decorative short hedge around a bed of taller vegetables.)

Basil is an annual plant easily started by sowing its seeds, either in containers indoors or directly into the garden. (See General Gardening Tips, page 79.) Prepare the garden by digging in generous amounts of compost or a packaged fertilizer with good amounts of nitrogen. Wait until the weather has warmed completely, nighttime temperatures are well into the fifties, and all danger of frost has passed before setting out young plants or sowing the seeds in the garden. Space the young plants about 1 foot apart—they need room to grow. (The smaller, bush types may be positioned closer together.)

Frequent cutting keeps basil from going to seed and dying prematurely. As soon as basil plants are 6 or so inches high and have more than one set of leaves, pinch off the top set. The plant will send out two stems, each of which will develop sets of leaves. Repeat the pinch when multiple sets develop on each stem, and the plants will grow full and leafy, instead of tall and sparse. (Globe basil will grow into a round shape naturally without being pinched.)

Basil is a tropical plant native to Africa, India, and Asia. It is extremely sensitive to cool temperatures (it's practically the first plant to die in the frosts of fall). Basil will even turn black in the refrigerator, so to keep cuttings fresh for a few days, set their stems into a glass of water on the kitchen counter.

The Most Italian of Herbs

OREGANO (*Origano*)

Oregano is a rangy, though attractive, plant with fuzzy little leaves, pretty white flowers, and hairy, square stems. Native to the Mediterranean region, it has an aromatic, peppery flavor that enhances almost every kind of food, including cheeses, eggs, meats, poultry, vegetables, and seafood. It's especially indispensable for tomato sauces, especially *salsa pizzaiola*, a thick sauce so named because it's made for topping pizza. Braised pork chops or steak *alla pizzaiola* are served with the sauce, too.

The best oregano can't be grown from seed. Even the seeds of a plant with a strong, true oregano flavor will most likely grow into a plant with a milder flavor, something that tastes more like mint than pizza. The best way to ensure true oregano flavor in the herb garden is to buy a small oregano plant that's been propagated from a cutting or root division of a good-tasting parent.

For planting, choose a spot with loose, average soil that drains well. As with the other Mediterranean herbs mentioned here, oregano's flavors will be more concentrated if the soil is not overly rich in nitrogen. Don't amend the soil with anything stronger than compost. Mounding the soil into a raised bed will help with drainage, too. (See General Gardening Tips, page 79.) Set the young oregano plant into its permanent home anytime after the danger of hard frost has passed. It's a hardy perennial and will survive most cold winters.

Begin to harvest a few leaves from the plant as soon as it begins to grow. Like most herbs, oregano will form a more attractive rounded shape and produce more tender leaves if it's cut back regularly.

Oregano

PARSLEY (*Prezzemolo*)

Parsley is the most frequently used of all of Italy's herbs, and Italian gardeners rig mini-greenhouses over their plants to ensure a supply of fresh leaves throughout the winter. The type of parsley most common in Italy is the broad-leafed kind (sometimes called "Italian parsley"). *Gigante D'Italia* is a robust variety of flat-leafed parsley that has big, tall stalks similiar to those of celery.

More flavorful and robust than curly-leafed parsley, broad-leafed parsley adds body and stamina to Italian soups, sauces, and salads. Two thousand years ago, Italian bakers added parsley to loaves of bread for flavor, and its use hasn't waned. It pairs especially well with the mild flavors of chicken and fish, and no soup seems complete without it. Parsley can be substituted for some or all of the basil in pesto, and it's the main green herb in *salsa verde*, the classic Italian green herb sauce that accompanies vegetables and meats.

Pasta with a sauce of chopped parsley and garlic steeped in warm olive oil is a simple, elegant dish often eaten by Italians too poor to afford anything else. (Those who can, add a little grated cheese.)

Parsley is a biennial—it is hardy enough to survive most winters, but will

The Most Italian of Herbs

flower and go to seed in its second year, losing flavor in the process. To have fresh, new parsley every year, buy little seedlings from an herb nursery each spring. Seeds can also be sown indoors in containers or directly into the garden (see General Gardening Tips, page 79). Parsley seeds can be a little slow to sprout, because they are naturally coated with growth-inhibiting substances. Rinse the seeds well in water before sowing them, then keep their growing medium moist. Parsley is cold-hardy, and young plants can be set out or seeds can be sown into the garden while spring days are still cool.

Unlike the other herbs mentioned here, parsley doesn't need regular trimming. The plants will grow full and bushy without it. Harvest the outer leaves first, and be careful not to cut into the tiny sprouting leaves at the central growing point of the plant.

ROSEMARY (*Rosmarino*)

Rosemary is a classic Mediterranean-area plant—its small, fleshy leaves are silvery gray, its stems are woody, and it thrives in well-drained soil and thick, moisture-laden mists from the sea. Its flowers are small, blue, and pretty and are much visited by bees.

Rosemary has a strong, piney flavor best combined with sturdy foods like pork, lamb, baked onions, and roasted potatoes. To prepare pork chops braised in wine, a dish from northern Italy, crushed rosemary and sage leaves (and garlic, of course) are pressed into the sides of the chops before they are browned in olive oil and butter.

Rosemary is easily started from seed (see General Gardening Tips, page 79). Small seedlings are readily available from plant nurseries, too. In late spring, set the young plants into average soil that drains well, and give them lots of water throughout the growing season.

Start pinching the tips of young rosemary plants when they get to be 6 inches tall or so. Trimming will cause the plant to branch out into many tender little twigs, forming a bushier plant. Rosemary will develop into a low perennial shrub in mild climates. In colder climates, chances of winter survival are improved by surrounding the plant with a thick mulch of straw or dried leaves.

SAGE (Salvia)

With its silvery foliage, sage is another true Mediterranean-region plant. The raspy, earthy flavor especially complements delicate veal. In *saltimbocca,* which translates as "jump into the mouth" because that's what they do, slices of ham and veal are seasoned with sage, then rolled up to be sautéed in butter and braised in white wine. Around Rome, veal chops are served with a sauce flavored with fresh sage, butter, and vermouth. And white beans flavored with sage is a classic.

Widely used in northern Italian cooking, sage stars in a simple pasta sauce (see Recipes, page 99, in the appendixes) prepared with a handful of small sage leaves sautéed in garlic and oil, and tossed over hearty pasta.

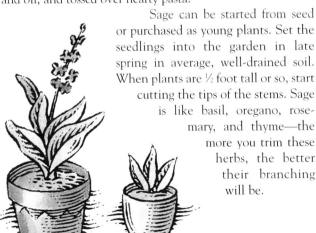

Sage can be started from seed or purchased as young plants. Set the seedlings into the garden in late spring in average, well-drained soil. When plants are ½ foot tall or so, start cutting the tips of the stems. Sage is like basil, oregano, rosemary, and thyme—the more you trim these herbs, the better their branching will be.

THYME (Timo)

Native to the Mediterranean region, thyme is a tough, low-growing, multistemmed plant with tiny leaves. Its sharp, strong flavor is particularly compatible with a variety of meats, in seafood stews and minestrone, and as a seasoning for sweet, bland vegetables such as carrots, cabbage, and onions. Thyme is often added to tomato sauces, too.

Start thyme by sowing its seeds in containers in spring or purchasing small plants from a nursery. Set the young plants into their garden bed of average soil (well drained, of course) in late spring. Start trimming the tender tips from stems of thyme when the plant is several inches tall.

Thyme is a hardy perennial that should have no trouble surviving most winters. Large plants have a tendency to die out in the center, but can be revived by division. Cut the old plant into sections with a sharp spade and replant the pieces in a new location.

The Most Italian of Herbs

GENERAL GARDENING TIPS

Good gardening practices are international, but the typical Italian plot has some characteristic features.

First and foremost is practicality. Every Italian garden worth its garlic has a compost pile where leaves and other plant waste materials that came out of the garden decompose before going back to the garden as organic fertilizer. Due to expense and tradition, chemical fertilizers were slow to be adopted by Italian growers, who used whatever they had on hand and recycled organic materials long before it became fashionable. Besides, each household once kept its own chickens and pigs, and manure was plentiful. Before being spread on the garden as fertilizer, manure was aged to a proper ripeness in the compost pile. Today Italian gardeners may buy their manure and mulching materials from garden stores, but old habits persist.

Next comes beauty. The world turned to Italy to see the classic standard of landscape design. The grand masters surrounded the great old villas with walls and borders, paths and portals, statuary and shrubbery to create garden rooms that brought the inside out. Some of these formal

General Gardening Tips

features often turn up in more modest forms in typical yards. In Italy, vegetable gardens are invariably surrounded by rough rock walls that are used to support the vines of tomatoes and squash. Attractive paths separate vegetable beds. Fig, pomegranate, and citrus trees divide production areas, and grape arbors form cool bowers for a gardener's rest.

Even the modern concept of edible landscaping, or designing a food garden to be as attractive as an ornamental planting, has deep roots in Italy, where it's not unusual to see formal beds of mixed colors and textures—for example, a checkerboard composed of alternate plants of bright green celery and dark green chard, bordered with dark red radicchio rosettes. And because space is often tight, a line of rose bushes might be interplanted with feathery fennel and other herbs in a formal, repeating pattern.

In general, Italian gardens are very neat, with not a weed in sight. Gardeners take great pride in how their outdoor rooms look. They take their gardening very seriously, at the same time enjoying it as a way to relax every evening.

As to the basics of gardening in any style, the following are some practical considerations, in chronological order of the garden's development.

SITING THE GARDEN

The ideal spot for a garden has a lot of sun, which is the source of the energy plants use to grow. Sunlight is especially important for vegetable plants, because the more sunlight they collect, the bigger and better their edible parts will be. That's why a sunny garden is a productive garden.

The best place for a garden, in terms of light, is a spot that is in sunshine from morning to night. Most light blockers can be divided into two categories: buildings and trees. Evaluate potential garden locations by checking for shade several times in the course of the day. At the very least, a vegetable garden needs about half a day of sunlight, or six to eight hours.

The best soil for a garden is one that is soft and crumbly, one that holds moisture but doesn't retain it, with not too much sand or clay. Perfection is not necessary: Any soil can be improved immensely with a little attention (and compost, see below).

DIGGING THE GARDEN

To create a garden in a spot where no garden has ever grown before, you'll probably need to clear the surface of some plants. If the site is in lawn, use a sharp spade to cut the sod into small, easy-to-remove pieces, pry them up, and stack them upside down in an out-of-the-way place. The grass will eventually die and the resulting pile of soil and dead grass debris can be added to the garden later.

Using a shovel and a spading fork, work the soil until it is loose and can be raked easily. (If the garden is large, use power tilling equipment to work the soil.) Pull out any roots, knocking as much soil as possible from them before placing roots and stalks in a pile to decompose. Remove as many rocks as possible and use them to delineate beds and walkways.

General Gardening Tips

RAISED-BED RATIONALE

Raised beds are simply areas where the soil has been mounded up so the planting surface is several inches above the surrounding soil. The spots from which the soil was removed become the walkways between the beds. Raising the planting area just a few inches allows the soil to drain more easily after rain and to warm up more quickly in spring.

Raised beds should be no wider than twice what the gardener can comfortably reach across. This means that the planting area is always accessible from outside of the bed, and the soil within the bed is never stepped on. This keeps the soil of the bed soft and uncompacted, allowing plant roots to penetrate easily and deeply.

SOIL FERTILITY

The soil that forms a garden is a mixture of organic (living or once living) and inorganic (rock and mineral) substances. To grow well, plants need a wide range of both types of materials.

Soils can vary widely in their chemical makeup, depending in part on geography and geology. A soil test will quickly determine if a particular soil has all of the necessary ingredients plants need to grow healthy. A few of the most important elements crucial for healthy plant growth are nitrogen, potassium, phosphorus, calcium, magnesium, and sulfur.

Many states provide inexpensive soil tests through their cooperative extension services, listed in the Blue Pages of the telephone book. Many of the soil-testing labs are associated with state universities. Independent soil-testing labs can also be located via the Yellow Pages. Test results will show the levels of the above elements in the soil, with recommendations for remedying any imbalances with fertilizers and mineral supplements.

COMPOST

Barring any extreme imbalances (which would show up in the results of a soil test), most elements essential to plant growth can be found in compost. Many municipalities now operate composting programs. These programs collect leaves, grass clippings, and other yard wastes, break them down through natural decomposition, and return the resulting natural fertilizer to municipality residents, free for the taking.

Of course, backyard composting is an old Italian tradition. Coffee grounds, droppings from the horses in the street and the chickens in the coop, the trimmings from the vegetables that went into the minestrone—all these bits and pieces of organic matter were mixed together in a pile to rot, then used to fertilize growing plants in the era before chemical fertilizers.

For fastest and most complete decomposition in a compost pile, organic materials should be mixed together in a ratio of about twenty-five parts of hard, brown, carbon-rich ingredients (wood chips, sawdust, small branches, fall leaves, pithy stalks, etc.) to about one part of soft, green, nitrogen-rich materials (grass clippings, green leaves, manure, plants past their prime, vegetable trimmings, etc.). Before mixing them together, chop up the materials as finely as possible. Keep the pile of organic matter moist but not

General Gardening Tips

soggy (it should feel like a wrung-out sponge), mix it up every couple of days or so, and when it all starts looking soft and brown and amorphous, it's finished compost. (Caution: Partially decomposed compost spread on the garden can tie up essential nutrients and disrupt plant growth.)

The equivalent of a 1-inch layer of finished compost dug deeply into garden beds before planting, or just spread on the surface around growing plants, is just about all the fertilizer an average garden needs to produce good crops.

SEED STARTING, POTTING MIXES, AND EQUIPMENT

Starting your own plants from seed is the only way to grow many of the truly authentic Italian varieties mentioned in this book. (Most American seedling nurseries just don't choose to grow Principle Borghese tomatoes or *Corno Di Toro* peppers.) It's really easy. All it takes is the seeds, a container to plant them in, and some growing medium to fill it. Containers for starting seed, as long as they have little holes in the bottom for drainage, can be anything from small flowerpots, to flat, shallow rectangles, to professional trays with many divisions to hold one plant each. Peat pots are time-saving little containers that get planted along with the seedlings they hold.

Special seed-growing mixes are sold at garden centers. They are light in texture (so germinating seeds can sprout easily) and retain moisture well. A good, do-it-yourself mix contains equal parts of vermiculite, perlite, peat moss, and finely sifted compost.

When it's time to plant the
seeds, fill a bucket or other container half full of the seed-
starting mix. Add water, and
stir until the mix is moist but not
sopping wet. Fill the planting con-
tainers almost to the brim with the moist mix, and smooth
the surface of the mix.

Drop seeds onto the moist mix, one per peat pot or
small tray division. In larger containers or flats without divisions, try to space the seeds neatly and evenly. Space larger
seeds (for tomatoes, peppers, and broccoli, for example) at
least 2 inches apart. Smaller seeds (herbs, etc.) can be
placed 1 inch apart. Cover the seeds with a fine layer of dry
seed-starting mix, and mist the surface gently with water
from a spray bottle.

Lay a piece of plastic wrap over the containers and set
them in a warm spot where the temperature stays somewhere
in the seventies. As soon as seeds start to sprout, remove the
plastic wrap and set the containers in a brightly lit spot. A
sunny windowsill that gets at least twelve hours of bright
light per day is a good place. Grow lights or fluorescent lights
a few inches away from seedlings are good, too.

Once the seedlings start forming leaves, feed them by
watering them with a weak solution of fish emulsion, seaweed extract, or compost tea every two weeks. (The first
two products are sold at garden centers; to make compost
tea, soak a small quantity of compost in water for several
days, then strain it.) Move the seedlings into larger containers if they need more growing room before it's time to
move them outdoors.

TRANSPLANT TACTICS

As daytime temperatures reach the sixties, it's time to start bringing the seedlings outdoors for longer and longer periods of time. (This is called "hardening off.") Start by setting the containers of seedlings outside for about one hour in a shaded, protected spot, and gradually work up to a full day in bright sun.

When it's time to give seedlings their permanent spot in the garden, dig small holes with a trowel or shovel, and gently set the seedlings in place. The date for moving plants outside (and their spacing in the garden) will vary for each vegetable; see specific instructions in the section for each vegetable.

Gardens are really combinations of types of plants: short, tall, spreading, or climbing. Locate tall or climbing crops across the north side of the garden so they don't block the sun from the shorter or spreading plants in the front of the garden.

DIRECT SEEDING

Some kinds of plants do best if their seeds are sown where they are to grow. Beans, for example, quickly outgrow little containers if started indoors; better to wait until it's nice and warm outside and all danger of frost has passed, then plant the bean seeds directly into the garden.

Follow instructions (in this book, on seed packets, or in seed catalogs) about how far apart to space the seeds. After the seeds sprout, pull out the smaller, weaker seedlings to give the healthiest, most vigorous plants the room they need. Giving plants enough room to grow really pays off. They grow larger and bushier, and they are less at risk from pests and diseases.

MULCHING

Covering bare soil around vegetable plants with an organic material such as grass clippings, straw, or dried leaves is a good way to prevent the growth of weeds. Mulch keeps the soil around plant roots moist and conserves water. As the mulch decomposes, it adds organic matter to the soil. It also fosters the growth of beneficial organisms, such as earthworms.

IRRIGATION

It is better to water a garden deeply and less frequently than to give it a quick shower more frequently. A thorough soaking penetrates to all the roots, not just the ones close to the surface. If plants are grown in raised beds in soil that drains well, overwatering is not a danger. However, some crops, including tomatoes, will form sweeter, more flavorful fruit if they are not given too much water after their fruits begin to form.

TRELLISING AND STAKING

Some vegetables (some very important Italian favorites, including tomatoes, beans, and squash) have long vines that develop best when given support to climb vertically. Fences are ideal supports; train the vines upright by gently weaving the tips of the vines farther and farther up the fence as they grow.

Beans can be planted around the bottom of a tepee made out of 8-foot bamboo stakes; wrap the leading bean tendrils around the stakes as the vines grow. Climbing beans can also be planted in a patch of corn. As the corn plants grow, the bean plants will curl themselves around the cornstalks and hang on for the ride.

Simple stakes, if they are strong enough, make good tomato plant supports. Tie the plant to the stake with twine or strips of fabric. When the tomato plant reaches the top of the stake, trim the top of the plant to encourage the growth of side shoots below.

Even some nonvining plants benefit from staking. Tie young peppers and eggplants to a sturdy piece of bamboo inserted into the ground next to the plants. Staking keeps plants upright in wind and rain, and also enhances the exposure of leaves to sunlight to improve yields.

PEST CONTROL

The best defense against insect pests and diseases is to grow plants as free of stress as possible. Strong, healthy plants that are fed and watered well have a better chance of fighting off attack and infection. What's more, strong plants just don't attract as many insect pests as weak, unhealthy plants.

Floating row covers are very light fabrics that let rain and sun pass through, but exclude harmful insects and protect plants growing beneath the fabric. Row covers are especially useful to keep caterpillar pests off broccoli, cauliflower, and cabbage. Arrange the row covers over young transplants as soon as they are set into place in the garden, leaving enough slack for the young plants to grow into. Anchor the edges of the row cover to the soil with boards or rocks.

Many pest insects can be kept in check by their natural enemies, sometimes called "beneficial insects." Ladybugs and lacewings are common examples of "good" bugs that eat "bad" bugs, but there are many more, such as tachinid flies, robber flies, spined soldier bugs, minute pirate bugs, parasitic wasps, predator wasps, ground beetles, and rove beetles, just to name a few.

One of the best ways to protect and encourage beneficial insects in the garden is to plant lots of flowers so that they have something to eat while they seek out pest insects. Plants that have tiny flowers are best—their pollen and nectar are within easy reach of tiny insects' mouths. Some of the best small-flowered plants to grow include umbels with flat flower heads—like dill, fennel, and Queen Anne's lace—and composites with shallow flowers—like daisies, cosmos, and coneflowers. Flowering herbs and mints are especially attractive to beneficials, too.

In addition to a full season of flowers, grow a variety of plants—such as shrubs, trees, perennial grasses, and ground covers—close to the garden to provide a range of habitats. A water fixture, such as a small pond or fountain or birdbath, will add diversity by attracting thirsty insects. And, of course, one of the best ways to help nature regulate itself is to refrain from using chemical pesticides.

APPENDIXES

RECIPES FOR THE
ITALIAN KITCHEN GARDEN

RUSTIC FENNEL

The Italian word for fennel is *finocchio*. If you eat too much of it, your nose will grow.

    1 tablespoon olive oil
    3 cloves garlic, minced
    3 cups sliced fennel stalks
    3 medium tomatoes, peeled, seeded, and diced
    healthy squeeze of lemon (optional)

Pour olive oil into a saucepan over medium heat. Stir in the minced garlic, but do not brown. Add the fennel and the tomatoes. Stir occasionally until the tomatoes begin to release their liquid, then turn down the heat, and allow to simmer until the fennel is tender (about 10 minutes). Serve as an accompaniment to meat, a salad of bitter greens, and hearty fresh bread.

Serves 4.

Flavor Tip: Fennel Grilled Fish
Wrap pieces of fish in a thick layer of green, feathery fennel leaves and grill them on a slow fire. Or dry the tougher upper-stem parts of the fennel plant (the segments between the bulbs and the leaves) and throw them onto the coals as you barbecue the fish, for a licorice-tinged smoky flavor.

MINESTRONE

In Italian, *minestra* is the word for soup, which is usually served as a first course. Minestrone is a big, catch-all term that generally refers to some version of vegetable soup that contains some kind of pasta or starch. Around Genoa, minestrone is made with meat stock, pasta, potatoes, lots of green vegetables like zucchini, leeks, green beans, peas, and cabbage, and is served topped with a spoonful of green pesto. Around Milan, minestrone contains rice. Other minestrones start with a bean stock base. This recipe uses freshly shelled beans, and is only a guide; feel free to substitute whatever is ripening in your garden.

½ cup chopped onion

2 cloves minced garlic

1 tablespoon olive oil

2 quarts water or stock (beef, chicken, or vegetable)

½ cup fresh shelled *cannellone* or Borlotto beans
(or substitute canned or cooked dried beans)

1 medium potato, diced

2 cups peeled, seeded, and chopped tomatoes, with juice

1 large carrot, sliced

1 stalk celery, diced

1 cup green and/or yellow Romano-type beans, cut in
1-inch lengths

2 tablespoons diced green and/or sweet red pepper

1 medium zucchini, diced

¼ cup shredded cabbage

½ cup small pasta

1 tablespoon each of chopped fresh parsley, basil, and
oregano

salt and freshly ground black pepper to taste

Sauté onion and garlic in olive oil. Add stock and beans and potatoes. When the beans and potatoes are half tender, about 15 minutes, add the remaining vegetables and simmer about 30 minutes. Add the pasta, and simmer until soft. Add chopped herbs and salt and pepper, and simmer a few minutes more. Serve with freshly grated Parmesan cheese.

Serves 8.

PESTO

Pesto is one of the many variations on green herb sauces (*salsa verde*) found throughout Italy. Its name derives from the old way of making it by crushing the ingredients by hand with a mortar in a pestle. Use pesto as a sauce for pasta, as a seasoning for soup, or any food in need of a dressing. This is the classic Genovese version; vary it by substituting fresh parsley for some of the basil.

2 cups fresh basil leaves, removed from their stalks
1 teaspoon salt
¼ teaspoon black pepper
2 cloves minced garlic
2 tablespoons pine nuts or English walnuts
½ cup olive oil
½ cup grated Parmesan cheese

Place ingredients in a blender or food processor and chop until all are finely blended. Stop to push the ingredients down, or add a little more olive oil, if necessary, to obtain a thick but saucy consistency.

Enough pesto for 1 pound of pasta that serves 4.

FRESH TOMATO SAUCE

This is the simplest of the simple: a delicate sauce made of fresh ripe tomatoes, seasoned with one or two herbs, and tossed with fresh pasta.

    3 tablespoons of extra-virgin olive oil
    1 medium onion, finely chopped
    4 to 5 medium, fully ripe tomatoes, peeled,
        seeded, and chopped, with juice
    salt and black pepper to taste
    1 tablespoon each fresh, chopped basil and parsley
    ½ teaspoon sugar

Sauté the onions in the olive oil until very tender. Add the tomatoes, salt, and pepper, and simmer about 30 minutes until smooth. Add the herbs and sugar, stir, and toss with 1 pound of hot, cooked pasta. Serve with freshly grated Romano cheese.

Serves 4.

Recipes for the Italian Kitchen Garden

SWEET PEPPER SAUTÉ

This recipe is a variation of *peperonata*, a dish containing peppers, onions, and tomatoes that can be served hot with a meal or cold with antipasto or meats.

6 large, ripe (or half-ripe) red or yellow sweet peppers
¼ cup olive oil
1 large sweet onion, sliced
6 cloves garlic, peeled and sliced
1 tablespoon roughly chopped flat parsley
freshly ground black pepper
½ pound fresh mozzarella cheese, cut into small cubes
1 tin flat anchovies
1 long loaf bread

Cut the peppers into 1-by-1-inch pieces, removing stems and seeds. Put the oil in a large sauté pan, and add the peppers, onion, and garlic. Sauté very slowly for about 45 minutes so the vegetables soften and slightly caramelize (turn brown) around the edges. Add the parsley, black pepper, and cheese, and toss quickly, then pour into a flat bowl. Cut the anchovies into 1-inch pieces and strew them over the pepper sauté. Serve beside a plate of toasted half slices of bread to be topped with the pepper mixture just before they're popped into the mouth.

Serves 8 as an appetizer.

PASTA WITH SAGE SAUCE

This is a variation on how Betty O'Toole, an herb grower in Madison, Florida, enjoyed sage in northern Italy.

    ¼ cup olive oil
    4 cloves garlic, sliced
    2 tablespoons butter
    ½ cup small, fresh sage leaves, cleaned and trimmed of
        stems
    1 pound long, thin pasta such as spaghetti or fettuccine
    freshly ground black pepper, salt to taste
    freshly grated Parmesan cheese
    dried red pepper flakes (optional)

Pour oil into pan. Gently sauté sliced garlic in olive oil until barely tan and toasty. Do not overcook. Add butter and sage leaves, and stir. Pour over cooked pasta, and add black pepper, salt, and cheese as you toss.

Serves 4.

STEAMED GREENS

1 pound greens (chard, spinach, kale, or broccoli raab)
1 medium onion, sliced
3 tablespoons olive oil
1 tablespoon balsamic vinegar
salt and freshly ground black pepper

Prepare the greens by washing well; chop any large stems into 1-inch pieces. Sauté the onion in the olive oil in a large pot for 3 minutes. Add greens and steam (the water clinging to the leaves should be sufficient to cook the greens). When the greens are limp and the water has evaporated, add the vinegar, salt, and pepper. Mix and serve.

Serves 4.

ACCOMPANIMENTS

Olive oil

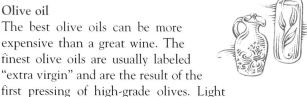

The best olive oils can be more expensive than a great wine. The finest olive oils are usually labeled "extra virgin" and are the result of the first pressing of high-grade olives. Light gold in color and fruity in flavor, extra virgin oils are best appreciated in dishes that don't mask their flavors, such as simple salads. "Virgin" olive oil is the first pressing of less perfect olives. A second pressing produces "pure" olive oil, which is darker and stronger. Both virgin and pure olive oils are wonderful for heartier dishes and cooking. Tuscany and Umbria are the Italian regions most renowned for their olive oils.

Vinegar

In a nation of vineyards, there are many different kinds of vinegar: red wine vinegar, white wine vinegar, and—the most revered of all—balsamic vinegar. It has a rich, dark brown color and adds complex sweet-and-sour flavor to salads and meat dishes. *Aceto balsamico* is also considered a tonic, a life-giving substance, and a treasure to be handed down from generation to generation. (*"Balsam"/"balsamico"* come from the same root as the word "balm," a healing substance.) The city of Modena in the Emilia-Romagna region is famous for its balsamic vinegar, which begins life as juice from grapes with a high sugar content. It's fermented and aged in wooden barrels a minimum of three years, but the very best can be fifty years old or more.

Cheese

As with wine and olive oil, cheese specialties are the pride of each Italian region. There are at least 100 different Italian cheeses, made from cow, sheep, goat, or water buffalo milk. They are part of practically every meal, or enjoyed all alone or with fruit for dessert. Most indispensable might be salty, sharp Parmesan, a hard cheese typically grated onto soups and salads or combined with pasta or sauces. Table cheeses, served separately or in meat recipes, include mild and creamy provolone, Fontina and Bel Paese, and pungent, blue-veined Gorgonzola. Cheeses like ricotta, similar to cottage cheese, and mozzarella, a soft light cheese indispensable on pizza, are mainly used in cooking.

Wine

Italy produces hundreds of varieties of wine—every geographic region has its specialty. The most widely recognized is Chianti classico, a dry red from Tuscany that is served with meats and pasta. *Barolo*—a mellow red that's best when aged a little—and *barbera*—a red that ranges from light to full-bodied—are both produced in the Piedmont region bordering France. Both go well with meat and game. Mild and delicate *Soave* is best with seafood or light pasta. It's perhaps Italy's best-known white and is produced in the northeast, around Verona. *Frascati* is the "table wine of Rome" and can vary from dry to sweet and from sharp to mellow. It goes well with chicken, pasta, and fish. Dessert wines include Asti Spumante, a lightly sweet sparkling wine from Piedmont, and Marsala, a dark, sweet wine from Sicily.

PRESERVING THE HARVEST

How to dry tomatoes
Start with thick, meaty, low-moisture tomatoes like Principe Borghese or plum/paste varieties. Slice them about ¼ inch thick and lay the slices on a cookie sheet coated with nonstick spray in a low (200°F) oven, or on the trays of an electric food dehydrator. When the tomato slices are crispy dry, store them in airtight jars. To rehydrate dried tomatoes, soak them in water, broth, or red or white wine for about 10 minutes.

How to dry herbs
To preserve herbs by drying, cut sprigs several inches long, tie their stems together with string to make small bunches, and hang them in a dry, airy, shaded spot. Alternately, lay cut sprigs or individual leaves on a tray or other flat container, cover them with a light material such as cheesecloth (paper towels will do, too), and place them in an out-of-the-way spot. A food dehydrator works well, also, but don't dry herbs in a low oven—the heat robs the essential oils of their strength. When the herb leaves are dry and crisp (they'll break instead of bend), remove them from their stems and store them in airtight jars. To preserve the most flavor, don't crush the leaves until adding them to recipes.

How to braid garlic and onions
Start with mature, freshly harvested onions or garlic. Rub off any loose soil and place the whole plants in an airy, shady place to dry. After several days, when the stalks are mostly dry but still pliable, trim the roots to about ¼ inch

from the bottom of each bulb. Wipe off any remaining soil and remove any loose bulb-wrapper leaves. Start the braid by holding three bulbs with their leafy stalks toward you. Make the braid by weaving alternate outer stalks over the center stalk. Add more bulbs one at a time, keeping them close together and two abreast. When the braid is as long as you want it (about 2 feet is manageable), secure the stalks with string to keep the braid from unraveling. Add a little loop for hanging in a cool, dry spot. Stored in this way, onions and garlic will last for months.

SEED and PLANT SOURCES

The following mail-order companies sell seeds for authentic Italian vegetables and herbs:

Abundant Life Seed Foundation
P.O. Box 772
Port Townsend, WA 98368

Berton Seeds Co. Ltd.
4260 Weston Rd.
Weston, Ontario
M9L 1W9 Canada

The Cook's Garden
P.O. Box 535
Londonderry, VT 05148

Pinetree Garden Seeds
P.O. Box 300
New Gloucester, ME 04260

Shepherd's Garden Seeds
30 Irene St.
Torrington, CT 06790

The following company specializes in garlic:
Filaree Productions
182 Conconully Hwy.
Okanogan, WA 98840

The following company sells artichoke plants:
The Natural Gardening Company
217 San Anselmo Ave.
San Anselmo, CA 94960

And these companies sell herb seedlings:
Mountain Valley Growers
38325 Pepperweed Rd.
Squaw Valley, CA 93675

Well-Sweep Herb Farm
205 Mount Bethel Rd.
Port Murray, NJ 07865

SEED SAVING

When Italian immigrants came to the United States, they brought seeds for their vegetable gardens with them. They planted the seeds, they traded them to their neighbors, and they saved them from this year's crop for next year's garden. In this way, many truly authentic Italian heirloom varieties have been preserved.

If this kind of gardening appeals to you, consider joining Seed Savers Exchange, a worldwide network of gardeners who grow their own seeds as they garden. Members sell seeds at nominal, standard costs to other members, who grow them, save the seeds, and offer them to other gardeners/seed savers, in turn. Typical seed descriptions in *The Seed Savers Yearbook,* the listing of members' offerings, contain phrases like "considered to be the very best tasting zucchini in Italy" or "oxheart tomato brought from Italy" or "Italian name means 'light green Romaine as sold by the greengrocers'."

To receive a color brochure describing *Seed Savers* projects and publications, send $1 and your address to *Seed Savers Exchange,* 3076 N. Winn Road, Decorah, Iowa 52101.

There's also a Canadian seed-saving organization. For information, write to *Seeds of Diversity Canada,* P.O. Box 36, Station Q, Toronto, Ontario, M4T 2L7 Canada.

FURTHER READING

The Italian Gourmet, by Giorgio Mistretta (Sedgewood Press, 1992). A beautifully illustrated book of delicate traditional recipes for authentic ingredients from the gardens of Italy.

Italy for the Gourmet Traveler, by Fred Plotkin (Little, Brown and Company, 1996). The specialties (and the customs and history) of each of Italy's regions, with blurbs on cities and towns, restaurants, bars, cafés, wineries, farms, food shops, cooking schools, bookstores, and more.

The Cooking of Italy, by Waverly Root and the editors of Time-Life Books (Time Inc., 1974). Part travelogue, part history book, the classic treatise on Italian cuisine.

Red, White and Greens—The Italian Way with Vegetables, by Faith Willinger (HarperCollins Publishers, 1996). Chockfull of horticultural history and asides, a book of recipes collected from wonderful Italian cooks, featuring Italian vegetables.

This book is dedicated to my mother,
who taught me how things grow.

ACKNOWLEDGMENTS

Thanks to Renee Shepherd, founder of Shepherd's Garden Seeds, who traveled to Italy each year ("gaining weight every time") to track down authentic Italian vegetable varieties for her seed company . . . to Vicki Sebastiani, co-owner with her husband, Sam, of Viansa Winery in Sonoma, California, which features an Italian garden, an Italian marketplace, and Tuscan barbecue . . . to John Gallo, the last Italian farmer in St. Bernard Parish, Louisiana . . . to Walter Berton of Berton Seeds . . . and to Omy, who waited.

ABOUT THE AUTHOR

Joanna Poncavage writes for leading gardening magazines. She also is the author of *Totally Sunflowers* (Celestial Arts, Berkeley, California), a book about those beautiful ornamentals, and *Grow a Totally Weird Garden* (Andrews McMeel Publishing, Kansas City, Missouri), a garden guide for children, and has contributed to publications of the *Brooklyn Botanic Garden*. She likes to grow garlic by the acre, and she has picked hot peppers until her fingers burned.